# Don't
# Ask

# Don't
# Ask

PHILIP LEVINE

*((*

**The University of Michigan Press     Ann Arbor**

Copyright © by The University of Michigan 1981
All rights reserved
Published in the United States of America by
The University of Michigan Press and simultaneously
in Rexdale, Canada, by John Wiley & Sons Canada, Limited
Manufactured in the United States of America
1988   1987   1986   1985   5   4   3   2

Library of Congress Cataloging in Publication Data

Levine, Philip, 1928–
    Don't ask.

    (Poets on poetry)
    1.   Levine, Philip, 1928–   —Interviews.
2.   Poets, American—20th century—Biography.
3.   Poetics.   I.   Title.   II.   Series.
PS3562.E9Z464   1981        811'.54 [B]        80-24992
ISBN 0-472-06327-8

# Acknowledgments

*Grateful acknowledgment is made to the following journals, publishers, and broadcast companies for permission to reprint copyrighted material:*

*American Poetry Review* for sections of "Touch Them Because They Gave Me My Life," an interview with Philip Levine, *American Poetry Review* 1, no. 1 (November-December 1972).

*Antaneus* for "An Interview with Philip Levine," *Antaneus*, Spring 1980.

Atheneum for the following poems: "On the Murder of Lieutenant José del Castillo by the Falangist Bravo Martinez, July 12, 1936," "New Season," "For the Poets of Chile," and "On the Corner" from *The Names of the Lost*, 1976. "Grandmother in Heaven" from *1933*, 1974. "Toward Home" from *7 Years from Somewhere*, 1979. "To P. L., 1916–1937" and "The Children's Crusade" from *They Feed They Lion*, 1972. All copyright © by Philip Levine.

*Australian Broadcasting Commission* for the interview with Philip Levine recorded in July, 1978, in Sydney, Australia, for the program "Books and Writers" by Jan Garrett.

*Michigan Quarterly Review* and David Remnick for portions of the interview with Philip Levine conducted December 31, 1978. Reprinted from the *Michigan Quarterly Review*, Summer 1980.

*Modern Poetry Association* for "To Cipriano, in the Wind" by Philip Levine from *Poetry*, September, 1979.

*Ohio Review* for "And See If the Voice Will Enter You: An Interview with Philip Levine," which first appeared in *Ohio Review* 16, no. 2 (Winter 1975).

*Parnassus: Poetry in Review* for "An Interview with Philip Levine," which first appeared in *Parnassus,* Spring-Summer 1978.

*Partisan Review* for "Poetry and Politics, an Interview with Philip Levine," which first appeared in *Partisan Review* 62, no. 1 (1975).

Station WFMT Chicago and Studs Terkel for "An Interview with Philip Levine," recorded March 13, 1977.

Stone Wall Press for "On the Edge" and "The Horse" from *On the Edge,* 1963, copyright © Philip Levine.

Wesleyan University Press for "Animals Are Passing from Our Lives" from *Not This Pig,* 1968, copyright © Philip Levine.

# Preface

Of what possible use or interest is this book? So many times having been asked my opinion I've answered honestly, "Who cares what I think?" I've changed my mind so many times about so many things that all that seems certain is that I'll change it again. So these interviews are full of contradictions, and I have left them that way to reflect who I am. One of my close friends who knows me as well as anyone refers to me as "a man out in the wind." I think I believe that that is where I should be, that to settle comfortably into any role, philosophy, world view, faith, would be a betrayal of who I was put on earth to be and what my poetry should be about.

"Who I was put on earth to be," is what I just wrote. Doesn't that suggest that there is some sort of faith, some sort of religion that I hold or that holds me? Well, so be it. Better poets than I have been Christians, Jews, practicing capitalists, orthodox atheists. Where is the church of this faith? I know it's not in the Vatican or on Wall Street or L.A.'s Miracle Mile. I would guess that if it's anywhere it's out in the wind.

With Keats I believe that the poet is the least po-etical of beings, and for similar reasons: he or she must be ready to enter whatever his eyes or his imagination put before him and to participate in the life of that *other*. So for those of you who read on, let me warn you: you won't find a man more sensitive than you, you won't find a light and airy spirit. I'm not a "special case." I'm a man who is more articulate than most people and one who found something called poetry quite early in life, grew to love it, determined to make it, and because of his stubbornness is some thirty years later still trying.

Frankly, I would prefer you read my poetry. I think it is a far clearer record of what I believed on those days during which I was most myself. True, it does not capture the everyday me, the guy who would answer my door with a drink in one hand and a baseball bat in the other, who might say depending on how the day had gone, "Enter and refresh yourself" or "Get the fuck off my porch." That is the man in this book. But of course they are one man, and perhaps that is useful to learn: that someone who could suffer and celebrate his life could slam his door in the face of creation, in the faces of those who crowd his poems, in your face.

How honest am I in these interviews? More honest, I think, than I ordinarily am. On each occasion I was aware that what I said might eventually find its way into print and into the hands of people whose good opinion I value. But that, you may be thinking, could be a motive for dishonesty. My friends, my children, the people I love, know me quite well, and I think they could certainly tell when I strayed from what I believe. In all fairness I know that this is not always the case. Recently a friend asked if I cared how reviewers responded to my poetry. Before I could answer my wife stated quite definitely, "No, he's above that!" In order to answer my friend, I had to contradict my wife. I simply said that my feelings were hurt when people did not like my poems, especially when those people were intelligent and sensitive. Both women looked so disappointed that I added that I'd never wept over a bad review or investigated the use of a hit man to deal with the star pupils of Yvor Winters, who seem especially to dislike my poems. Let me say that as far as I know there are no lies in these interviews, but my memory isn't as sharp as it once was, and like most people I want to be liked.

But I do not have to be liked, and there are many people whose dislike I do everything in my power to encourage. Let me tell a little tale, which happens to be true, which I think will clarify what I mean. When I was sixteen years old I had a close friend named Buddy Graham. I would guess he was between twenty-five and thirty years old. It was 1944, and he had recently been discharged from the army, although the war was not over. His was a restless nature, and there were very few men around his own age, so we became friends. One afternoon he came to my house and asked me to go swimming with him. He had a car, which I did not, and I enjoyed his company, so I went. When we arrived at the swimming pool of his choice I spotted a sign out in front which read, "No Jews, Niggers, or dogs allowed." Buddy and I were both Jewish by birth, and so I was startled that he seemed eager to enter the place. I pulled him to one side and asked him how he could go in. He answered calmly in a sort of night club Jewish accent, "I should ruin my life just because people hate me."

Over the years I've been asked repeatedly to write

critical pieces or give lectures on the relationship between poetry and cannibalism, early retirement, anarchy, the menstrual cycle, fasting, the gold standard. I've always declined these invitations even when they were well meant, not because I think such essays are useless—although in the main I think they are—or because I am lazy—which I'm not. I am a very superstitious man, so much so that I have a fear of formulating certain of my beliefs for fear of losing them. When asked what kind of God I believe in, I usually leave the room. When asked why poetry matters, I usually lie and say that without it the sun would not rise. I do not understand why the trees and vines my wife plants grow with a ferocity that seems like joy, nor do I question them. I pluck the plums and grapes and quench my thirst in the heat of summer. I spent most of my growing up doubting the value of everything and disbelieving all I was taught. At twenty-two I found myself a very cynical young man, one who drank enough to suggest he didn't even value his own body, and then proved it by driving a '48 Pontiac at horrendous speeds. I am no longer that young man. I coast soberly through stop signs and believe and do not question. If the grass grows, so can I.

I've been called a poet of desolation—of a world without solace—and I know that many people read my poetry that way. It was not my intention to write such a body of poetry, but it was also not my intention to stop growing before I reached 5′10″ or to become fifty-one in such a short time. I believe these interviews will make it clear that I am here, alive and OK, because I want to be and not out of fear of what comes after. As I mention in the interview with Calvin Bedient, I often clown around during poetry readings, and although I know it annoys many people, I do it for particular reasons. Some of that same buffoonery is in these interviews and for the same reasons I gave Calvin. It's harder to catch it on the page than it is at a reading or in conversation, but I would remove too much of what I enjoy here if I were to edit it out, so at times you must be prepared not to take me seriously.

I think these interviews make it clear I'm an intensely political person, but a man without a party, who—if things keep going as they are—may soon be a man without a country. I chose not to include one long interview conducted by two young political activists, for although it clarified many of my political attitudes and the roads that led me to them, it was unspeakably boring. I recall one question that went, "So you worked in automobile factories not to form cadres of the working class." And I answered, "I did it for the money." That was a high point of the interview since for the most part in those sentences we were speaking English. Let me be clear. When I refer to myself as an anarchist I do not mean to invoke the image of a terrorist or even a man who would burn the deed to his house because "property is theft," which I happen to believe is true. I don't believe in the validity of governments, laws, charters, all that hide us from our essential oneness. "We are put on earth a little space," Blake wrote, "That we may learn to bear the beams of love." And so in my poems I memorialize those men and women who struggled to bear that love. I don't believe in victory in my lifetime. I'm not sure I believe in victory at all, but I do believe in the struggle and preserving the names and natures of those who fought, for their sakes, for my sake, and for those who come after. If what Gabriel Celaya wrote is true, that *"Poesia es un arma cargada de futuro"* (Poetry is a weapon loaded with the future), then perhaps I too fought.

---

A careful reader or listener will find a great many changes from the original published or broadcast interviews, for which I do not apologize. Some of these versions are actually closer to what was said than the previously published interviews, which were often edited to suit the needs of the magazines in which they appeared. More often I have cut out certain parts which tended to be repeated in interview after interview, for as I said in the final interview what troubles me most is not that I was asked the same questions over and over, but that I gave the same answers no matter what the questions were. In some cases, as with the interview with Glover Davis and Dennis Saleh and the later one with David Remnick, very small portions of the original interviews seemed interesting, and so I've retained only those portions. With the broadcast interviews I faced another problem: I often tend to develop a line of thinking very slowly and by a somewhat incantatory process of repeating every banality several times; in preparing them for publication I reduced that to a single stream of banalities. In every case I tried my best to stick to the spirit and meaning of the original no matter how distant that was from my current beliefs.

# Contents

# Interview with Glover Davis
# and Dennis Saleh

Fresno, California, Spring, 1972

*Are you surprised that you've been in Fresno so long? That you've made it so well here coming from a place like Detroit?*

Well, I would say the thing that I think is so fitting is that coming from a shit hole like Detroit, it's perfectly beautiful that I should have wound up in a shit hole like Fresno. (Laughter) I think that's one of the reasons I'm comfortable here. I've never been really comfortable on the coast; San Francisco always seems a bit too polished for my style. I had a kind of style coming from Detroit that was perfect for Fresno even though it was a couple thousand miles away and it was urban and this was semirural. There was a certain correspondence, the hard edge and the nastiness of this pig pen. It was very easy to go on writing about Detroit in the context of Fresno because I'm surrounded by the same kinds of contrasts, a city whose vitality depended on exploited people who live like shit while there were the suburbs of the rich who enjoyed their privileges and had absolutely fixed the situation so it could never change. Just as the Poles and the blacks in Detroit could never own the factories, so the Chicanos in this valley and the poor whites could never own the farms and the vineyards and distilleries; it was the same kind of gross example of American capitalism. I just knew where I was, I was home. I was not tempted; I wasn't lured into some mid-kingdom where I could hobnob with the great because I was a poet. When I was up at Stanford for a year on a grant it was very seductive: "Oh, you write so well, why don't you come to my house. . . ." And I'd be eating with the rich. And you knew you were a slob basically, but you didn't quite know where you were, people were sort of petting and combing you . . .

*Rich people?*

Yeah, well, I guess so. You didn't know what they were. Their money wasn't showing. You were just eating it and drinking it and sitting on it, but in Fresno that never happens. The rich here are so gross and stupid they don't give a shit about poetry, they just want to have more speedboats and stuff like that. It's very much like Detroit. If you're *really* rich you're going to buy a ballclub, you're going to own the Detroit Lions and get all those jackasses to run back and forth on your lawn (laughter) and play in your private park. Same as Fresno. If you're really rich you've got 6,000 Chicanos to work in your garden.

*I'm interested in something. I'm interested in what happened when you went to Spain. The whole influence that Spain had on your poems. If you'd want to talk about that.*

I think that in the year before I went I was becoming somewhat dissatisfied. I don't know if that's quite the way to put it. There were changes taking place in me. Some of the poems I wrote just before I left make that clear, a poem like "Red Dust" or "Waking an Angel," a poem I wrote shortly before I left and really didn't quite understand or understand where it came from. I think I was kind of open and susceptible to influences. I think a lot of people could go to Spain and live for a year and very little would happen to them, but I was at a certain period in my life, my late thirties, I was passing from youth to middle age, and I was kind of open.

I was also like a lot of people or poets who hadn't been celebrated much, the guys who live outside the centers of celebration, here in a place like Fresno. I had a kind of arrogance and pride in how good I was, which I needed because I wasn't celebrated. Not that I went around crowing—I was quiet—but I had a lot of confidence in myself and in the way I wrote, and a firm belief that I knew who I was: I was this poet who was developing slowly and steadily toward some kind of aim.

And I went over to Spain and my life was very different. I had an enormous amount of leisure time and I was with my children in a way in which I hadn't been with them before, all the time, I was with my wife in a way I hadn't been with her before, and there were all these new experiences coming in, one after another, for a whole year. And it had a tremendous impact on me. There was the struggle to learn the language, there was the struggle to come to terms with the values of the people, with their explosions into emotion, with their indifference to me, their indifference to America, their indifference to my poetry and my identity as a person. A whole lot of things I had suddenly to grope with, to struggle with. I think the landscapes and the cities and the people, the way they looked and the way they behaved and the way they spoke were probably the most powerful things, and I was enormously open at that time in my life. It shook me up and changed me. There was the different climate, the different skies, different foods, different people, everything, and I was very unsure of myself suddenly. Kind of staggering in front of all this, and my habit for fifteen years at least had been to cope with things through poetry. What was difficult to cope with in my immediate range of experience, what was distressing or disturbing out there and within myself I somehow dealt with in a poem and kind of exorcised the terror of and came to terms with. And now there was too much for me to do this with, and I really felt burdened, frightened . . .

*In that* Naked Poetry *essay you say you didn't know what was happening, what was going on, inside or outside yourself . . .*

Yeah, I had the good luck, and I think it was luck, to weather it, gradually to feed it into me. By the end of the year the landscape seemed me, seemed like a projection of my own inner being. I felt that when I looked at the Spanish landscape I was looking at a part of myself. When I heard people speak I thought they were saying things that I was going to say, when I looked at their faces I thought I was looking in a mirror. In a year I began to become

Catalan in a small way. I felt a great sympathy for the people; they looked familiar to me. I think half of them are Jews anyway, and they look very Jewish. They look a lot like me.

They would come up on the street and speak to me, and I was learning the language and had a pretty fair accent, and in a while it didn't seem that foreign. It was a struggle. But in a way it was one of the things in my life I was lucky about. I didn't struggle too much. I accepted defeat. And through this I kind of triumphed, I became part of this place. And I think Franny helped me a lot. She felt tremendous sympathy with the place and the people, and very quickly—being a very winning kind of person, an attractive person—she made a lot of friends among the Spaniards. So that what at first seemed terrifying became in a while myself.

*Did you write a lot then, that first year?*

I had a pretty good year. That was the beginning of a kind of second phase in my writing life. I began to write a lot more. Up to '65, the first year I went to Spain, there was a limited amount to what I wrote, and suddenly I was writing twice as much. Or three times. Even later when I came back to teaching. It was a good year, and my poetry began to change. I think that what I was beginning to learn, not just to articulate but to learn, was that there were things in me that would create poems and I would just have to follow them, and I began to write less from a sense of identifying myself, "This is Philip Levine, this is the way he talks, this is the way he structures a poem." I was sort of listening to things as they came out and I followed them.

*Do you think that kind of experience, those terrifying experiences were coming, or did they just occur because you went to Spain. Could it have happened in Fresno?*

I don't know. More frightening things have happened in Fresno, since. My sense of who I am has been shaken even more. I think my poetry has continued to change without such powerful influences from the outside. The main things have been within me. It's very hard to go back and say, What would you have done if you hadn't? But my feeling is that it didn't actually require Spain.

*Maybe you're lucky that those things began in Spain, maybe you were able to deal with them easier there.*

Well, one of the things that happened the second time in Europe was that I was sick, I had a lot of illness, and I was a person that had never been sick in my whole life, and that was a great shock to me. It upset me profoundly. I'm a person who tends to define myself in certain ways, I needed definitions of who I was, and one of the things I was was *not* sick. Suddenly I was sick and lying in bed a lot of the time, weak, defenseless, and I'd always been a kind of person who was aggressive and thrusting myself into the world. Suddenly I was asking the world not to be thrusting, as long as I was sick I wanted the world to be passive for a while. "As long as I'm sick let's all be passive."

*Is "Salami" a poem out of that?*

No, it came before the sickness. It's a poem of recollection of the first time I lived in Spain, although it was written the second time I was there.

*There's something devastating that happens in the "Salami" poem. I don't know if the reader ever knows what it is, but when you talk about illness and being wasted, it sounds like "Salami."*

It's actually a kind of commingling of two experiences. One, a strange night in which I awakened—this was the second time I was in Spain—with a terrible nightmare. That's not true. It wasn't a nightmare. I woke up feeling very strange and right away I got out of bed, the bed felt wrong, and I went to the bathroom. Suddenly I felt seized by a physical force and thrown on the ground, and I saw this kind of luminous creature. We were struggling together, and I remembered Jacob and the angel, and I felt very much as though I was in that kind of situation, struggling with this, and then I felt that I was dying. I felt something like death coming over me, an enormous agony, a physical agony, I'd never experienced such incredible pain, like everywhere in me. Especially my head. My brains. An enormous howling. I was trying to howl but I couldn't, I didn't have the strength left. It passed. It was like a seizure, and I didn't understand what it was.

*Did you lose consciousness?*

No, never. I lay awake for the rest of the night; this happened at about four in the morning, and I just lay awake, afraid to sleep. My older brother was visiting me at the time. We hadn't talked to each other much for many years. I was lying in bed the next day, kind of rocky and wasted, and he came over, and he was very touched to see me this way. And he sat there on the other bed most of the day, and he talked, for the first time he talked about the war—he'd been in the air force during World War II, and there are details in "How Much Can It Hurt," you know, the bomber over Dresden, "my brother in his uniform," and all that . . .

*You said "Salami" was a kind of commingling of two experiences . . .*

Yeah, I had another experience the first time I lived in Spain, I really don't want to talk about it. And the two experiences had a great deal in common . . . and they wound up in the poem. The woman making the salami came from the first time I lived there, and the stone cutter I met. And I had this terrible fear of my son dying, my youngest son, which I talk about . . . "lying on a bed of colorless light" . . . and I ask if he's dead, "asleep or dead," I say. I had had this fear that he would die over there, that was the first time I was over there.

*Was something happening to Teddy?*

Yeah, he was having a lot of asthma attacks which made his breathing difficult, so frequently we would go in in the middle of the night to hear how he was breathing. He'd get frightened by it, so would we; it wasn't all that dangerous but it scared him. All those things come into the poem.

*"How Much Can It Hurt" was a poem I was going to ask*

*about. It's interesting to think about those two poems to-gether. I wouldn't have.*

The "Salami" poem was very quickly written. About three months later I was lying in bed one morning—I have very good hearing—it had been storming, and I'd usually wake up in rough weather and hear the sea, which I lived about a half a mile from. There'd been terrific storms when I'd gone to bed. When I woke it was very quiet and calm. I listened carefully, the sea wasn't crashing on the shore, and suddenly I heard a crow—it flew over—I heard this single caw of the crow. That's the way the last part of the poem begins: "a single crow passed. . . ." I just sort of got that in my mind, and the thing began to reach out. It was one of those times you know you're going to write a poem, and it's going to be a poem that's going to carry a lot of yourself.

*Jung says, somewhere, I forget where, that a whole part of your life comes together in a dream like that, and usually it's at the end, when this whole experience is over with. A dream like that is a kind of image of what you've been going through.*

This wasn't a dream. I was awake, completely, I'd turned on the lights. It was not even in the dark. That's what made it so frightening.

*I wrote a poem about you and something like that happened in it. You're turned back, you know, to the earth, to physical things. You don't want to be though. Like when I thought of you I thought there'd be a way in which it would be painful for you, but that's one of your purposes, to consider the basic things, though you didn't want to, you wanted to . . .*

Have an easier existence?

*Not easier. I didn't mean easier. Not that you wanted anything easy . . .*

Yeah, up there where you *will,* you *want,* where you're conscious, where you think you make choices, you choose the easy thing. It may turn out to fuck you up and add difficulty because you're ignorant, you know, so you blunder your way into your most significant experiences. I think most of the time you try to avoid what turn out to be your most important experiences. Which shows you how futile your choices are. I mean the whole notion of choice is kind of silly. You choose A because you think it's going to be easier, so you get in your car and drive away from the experience with your mother which might be painful, but of course the car hits a tree (laughter) and you have to experience what it's like to die. Or to suffer enormous pain. Or to kill somebody else. Yeah, a guy runs away from an experience he thinks will be terrible, so he has to live with the actuality of flight, disorientation.

*What's the biggest change in your writing from your first book to* They Feed They Lion?

I want to be a poet of joy as well as suffering. If you look at *On the Edge* you find the poetry of someone on the edge, on the edge of despair, the edge of breakdown, on the edge of his culture, of his own life. The image of fatherhood in that book is the image of the father, scared, hovering over the sick child, and furious at creation for afflicting the child. I think later I'm more likely to cherish the child no matter what he is. It's another attitude. Like I mean in "Salami" where the child gives to me, prays for me in sleep, and each one of his breaths is a prayer for me. Instead of me holding the child, keeping him alive, now I come close to death and the child gives me life. Fathers get their lives from their children; they don't hover over the little creatures forever. Of course my life was harder when I wrote the first poem. My son John had come close to dying.

*You feel the lion book is more affirmative?*

Yeah. I think the title poem, "They Feed They Lion," is a celebration of anger, which I love. In the poem "Breath" I celebrate my breathing, my living . . .

*That's the very last thing in the book, the song going out . . .*

Yeah, . . . my breath goes out, and my song goes with it in my lousy voice, which is also my poetry. I think the book is full of small celebrations of the things I see. I don't organize them or muster them to make harsh statements all the time, I just sort of touch them because they gave me my life. I think the book's much less thematic than my earlier books.

*You're leaving these things alone and just sort of showing them? I'm thinking of a poem like "Thistles," where things are just shown or revealed, and maybe you say very little about them.*

Well, that's the hope, that they're so much in themselves that they don't need me.

poet as channel

# Interview with Arthur E. Smith

Fresno, California, Fall, 1974

*In judging a poem, do you take into consideration the poet's attempt, along with his finished product, or is it simply a matter of the best achieved poetry? Does ambition come into the picture at all?*

Of course. That goes without saying. One of the most attractive qualities about a poem is its ambition. And I think that people rise to the occasion and that the best writing is really in the most ambitious poems.

*How do politics fit into a poem? I know that you're a political person, and yet your strongest poems are not concerned with politics at all. They are about people, individual persons who are lonely, depressed, on the verge of giving up—and yet holding on with a stubborn tenacity. This isn't politics, is it?*

Sure.

*How so?*

You're defining politics in a very narrow sense, as

having to do with political parties. I think the writing of a poem is a political act. We now exist in the kind of a world that Orwell was predicting, and the simple insistence upon accurate language has become a political act. Nothing is more obvious than what our politicians are doing to our language, so that if poets insist on the truth, or on an accurate rendition, or on a faithful use of language, if they for instance insist on an accurate depiction of people's lives as they are actually lived—this is a political act. You couldn't possibly make a movie about the way people live in the United States and show it to the Republican party and find them liking it. They would find it an intensely political movie. And they'd be right, it would be a political movie. The fact that a poem deals with the kinds of . . . I mean, what are the sources of anger in a lot of the poems that I write and a lot of other people write? The sources of anger are frequently social, and they have to do with the fact that people's lives are frustrated, they're lied to, they're cheated, that there is no equitable handing out of the goods of this world. A lot of the rage that one encounters in contemporary poetry has to do with the political facts of our lives. So I don't see that there is any real conflict here. I think being a poet is, in a sense, a political act—that is, if you're a real poet, not just a kind of court singer. If you're somebody who wants to go to the White House and amuse people, if you're the Sammy Davis of poetry, the Rod McKuen, obviously even that's a political act, an act of lackeyism.

*You would define politics in a broader sense, as Vallejo or Neruda did?*

Sure. You can define it in a number of ways, but certainly they are great political poets, and if you'll look at Vallejo you'll find that he never tells you how to vote, he never really talks about a political party. Occasionally he mentions that X is a Red, and as such he's shot, but by and large that's not what he's concerned with—he's concerned with the agony of living. One of the main reasons of living, why it's so agonizing, is that people with power have no compassion. And the minute you make that statement, it's an enormously political statement, and it describes our country as well.

*I notice that in the poetry of Hernandez or Vallejo or Neruda, when they narrow that political definition down into a particular party or person, it's usually a weaker poem.*

I don't remember Vallejo or Hernandez writing that kind of programmatic poetry. They may have, but I'm not aware of it. I know, for example, in the late Vallejo, some of the poems are magnificent and they are war poetry, poetry trying to raise the spirits of the people. This is true in Hernandez also. For example, he has a poem in which he says that his breath, that which animates him, which gives him his language, and his words and his mouth—this spirit is the same desire for worth and animation of the people. And he talks about the Spanish people and their refusal to bow down to be sheep, and their insistence on living life as a full human being rather than (and he uses the image of a gelded creature) the ox. And then at the end of the poem he says something like, "If I have to die, let me die with my head held high, dead, twenty times dead, with my mouth closed on the rough grasses." He then has the image of a nightingale, "There, among the rifle fire, where our struggle is, there are nightingales singing," which is the image of the poet. You make song among those who fight. It is true that Neruda wrote some ugly, stupid, boring—mainly boring—hymns to Stalin. They were boring and naive, but when you take a look at the immense range of poetry the guy wrote and you single out a couple of shitty poems, and those poems are named over and over again as a sort of example of what happens when you become political, I think it's a real mistake. I think that that political power he took into himself and lived so intensely animated hundreds of lines of great poetry, and if he wrote a couple of clinkers, they shouldn't be held up as examples of what happens when a poet becomes political. All men must be political, obviously, if we're going to live in a community that's worth living in, and poets are no exception. Poetry is not outside the mainstream of our lives, and if you take it outside, then it seems to me to be something less than vital.

*Spanish poets, the very good ones, can write about a Spanish people and produce a really good poem, and I fail to see that in many American poets. You have to speak individually, or else sound fatuous.*

I think you're wrong. Whitman talks about a people, and he's our greatest poet. Most of us don't talk directly about a people but we imply the people when we use the individual case. Our languages are different. But it is true that we have a harder time making the kind of general statements, and making them with authority. And when you look at the lives of many American poets you'll find that they are very alienated, all the way back to Emily Dickinson. So maybe we don't all feel that we speak for the people.

*Do you feel any compulsion to be socially responsive to any group or movement? Do you feel any social obligation to black, Chicano, Indian or women poets? There are some fine women poets in this country, but they have been played down and sometimes ignored. As a result of this, do you personally take a longer, more thorough look at books of poetry by women?*

Women in America have been writing marvelous poetry for a long, long time, and I'm not at all sure that they have been slighted. They haven't been by my tastes. I think that with blacks and Chicanos—and Indians I suppose, although I really don't have many acquaintances among Indians—something else has taken place that isn't so much in the awarding and the judging. It is something that takes place in their education where they are told that they can't write. It's as simple as that. They are discouraged from writing, so that you don't have Chicano poets to speak of until rather recently. They endured a school system which conspired, I think consciously, to tell them they could not write and even if they could learn to write they wouldn't write anything sophisticated or interesting enough to ever please this tremendous audience. They were discouraged in both cases from using their own language. In fact, they were told that they were illiterate. Blacks and Chicanos were told they don't have a language. Consequently, if their language is taken away from them, it is almost impossible for them to write.

*In other words, they are bilingual and yet have neither language?*

No, they are not bilingual. Black people may become bilingual in America if they want to get jobs at MIT or at advertising companies. They speak a language which is a form of American English, which they are told is not a form of American English, but a shit, fucked-up language, bad language—but it is a perfectly articulate language with its own rules of grammar and in many cases it has a lot more vitality and expressiveness than the main WASP language. We are constantly borrowing from it. I notice that my kids, ever since they have been in school, have come home with black expressions that have a lot of vitality and snap, just as I did when I was a kid. We borrowed heavily from black language, just as we have been borrowing black music and black poetry and the blues and folk songs—and telling these people that they don't have a language and they don't have a music and they don't have a song and they don't have a culture. They've known otherwise. And they've gone on composing, writing and making great art. And we now pick up books that are written in black language and we recognize that it's poetry. We know that Etheridge Knight is a tremendous poet. We know that Lucille Clifton is a fine poet, and . . . but that is recent. It seems to me that it's a very good thing. Thank God it's taking place. I see here, locally, a lot of very gifted Chicanos writing—a really vital literary movement. Part of the impetus comes from the fact that there is so much Chicano experience that as yet has not received its poetry, so that now there is this tremendous rush to give it the poetry it deserves. I find it one of the most vital movements, perhaps the most vital movement, in contemporary American poetry. I'm dazzled by how much good Chicano poetry there is being written by people who are really very young, still in their twenties. Now whether or not I am going to pick up every book by a black or a Chicano or an Indian or a woman and say, "Wow, I owe this book something," I don't know that I'm going to do that. I'm going to start reading the book and if I'm enthralled and excited by it, then I'm going to be enthralled and excited by it.

*I was going to use the example of Sylvia Plath. Not that she was so ignored during her life, but she wasn't that recognized either. In fact, she didn't publish many of her good poems until after her death. Not many people were interested in them even when she was sending them out.*

I think that's untrue. She was immensely successful—not successful in the way she became successful, which is really unlike the success of most poets. After she died she became a celebrity, but that's something else. I think as a poet she was very successful. She was younger than I and she was much more successful than I. I knew her work and I liked her work. The minute I saw the poems that were to wind up in *Ariel* I was enormously intrigued and excited by them, and so was everyone else I knew who read poetry.

*Robert Bly said in an interview in the* San Francisco Book Review *that if a poet is good and is writing good poetry, then for God's sake, leave him alone. Don't give him prizes and awards and money. These, if nothing else, will destroy him.*

In general, that's probably true. Although I'm not going to name anybody who has been destroyed by a prize—except for Tony Curtis and Marlon Brando. (Laughter) All the movie stars, all the movie stars. . . .

*Speaking of Bly, he's beginning to exert some influence at least among some younger poets through his magazine the* Seventies, *and of course there's the Black Mountain school—*

I'd like to interrupt you. Bly began exerting influence on whatever a younger poet is back in the fifties. The magazine was originally called the *Fifties.* And it was much more exciting in the fifties and sixties than it is now. How many issues have there been in the seventies?

*One, as far as I know. . . .*

That's right. So it's hardly a very vital magazine. Most of us know what he has to say. His contribution has been immense, but I don't think that it is very strong in younger people. I've seen a great reaction against it, for reasons I don't entirely understand.

*His poetry isn't all that strong, and yet he seems to—*

I disagree. He's a very strong poet.

*He had very weak moments in his last book. But his magazine—*

There are really weak moments in Whitman, weaker moments in Whitman than there are in Bly. Some of the worst poems you could ever read were written by Whitman, also some of the greatest. Whether Bly's last book was up to his best, I don't know. I don't happen to think it was his best book either, but he's still a tremendous poet, and a lot of the authority of the magazine comes from the fact that you know you are being addressed by a tremendous mind, a tremendous spirit, a tremendous poet. The spokesman before Bly was Rexroth. Maybe they shared it for a while. Obviously, there's going to be a new spokesman. Bly had an immense influence in the fifties and sixties, but I don't really know that he's going to be the influential figure of the seventies. I would think not. I would think it would be somebody else, a younger person. . . .

*Getting back to the schools of poetry, the Black Mountain school, the New York school, the Iowa workshop. . . . You have managed to remain somewhat aloof from all of these. Your poetry hasn't seemed to have been particularly influenced by any certain school.*

I have been influenced by a great many people who write poetry. I remember reading Allen Ginsberg back in the fifties when I was at Iowa, and liking him better than anything anyone was liking at Iowa. Iowa wasn't a school, it was a university. There wasn't a school of poetry there then. I haven't kept up with what's happening there since and I don't have any particular interest to. There was some real similarity in the Black Mountain poets, but I think what poets give each other is sympathy, and careful reading and honest criticism. I've taken from wherever I could find it. I read a lot of prose writers and try to learn from them. If you looked at almost all the good poets you would find that this is true. There are poets around who are recognizably, say, Black Mountain. I really don't—I take all that back. I really don't know what a Black Mountain poet is, except that I know some people who were at Black Mountain. If you showed me a poem and said, "Is this a Black Mountain poem?" I couldn't tell you. I'm not that interested in movements. Poetry is something that takes place alone, in solitude, in silence. And then there are these social relationships that people work out. They live in New York and so they become. . . . They have these friends. They are influenced as much by their friends' behavior and dress as they are by their poetry. Poetry comes out of the whole life and goes back into the whole life. Here I live in Fresno, and have for a long time. There was no real group of poets here, and so if I don't sound like a Black Mountain poet or a New York poet, it's small wonder really. And my influences have changed as I grow older. My tastes have changed and so my poetry has changed. I don't read the magazines with any faithfulness. I don't really know what's being written in America. This year reading all these books is a kind of welcome thing for me—to find out what's being written in the country.

*Maybe what you've been saying so far is the reason why you haven't been influenced by any particular style of writing.*

I have an idea of the kinds of poems that I want to write. I don't have a clear idea what they are, but I have an idea. Sometimes when I write a poem I think, "That's it! That's what I want." So I do have a kind of conception of what a poem ought to be. I don't know where it came from, and I think it's very old in me—all the way back to my teens probably, and it's been modified and changed with my experiences as a guy living in particular places and particular times, and my reading experiences. This is true for most of us. I think this "schools" thing is a way of dealing with poetry without reading. That is, if I pick up one of those books over there and I begin to say, "Unhuh, New York," well I can dismiss a book then without really coping with what it might be saying, without its challenge to me. I might pick up one of those books, read it, and say, "My heavens, this guy is doing things I never thought of doing, and it's really interesting. Maybe I ought to become a different kind of poet." That's a powerful experience. Or I might learn something. A guy might start talking about a particular subject: the stars, flowers, his neighbor, and I might suddenly be shocked into my deadness to the stars, flowers and my neighbors. But if I don't want to have a poetic experience, I can pick up the goddamn book and say, "Unhuh, Iowa," and slip it in a pigeonhole. "Ah, beat, hip, Black Mountain. . . ." I'm just not interested in reading that way. It's a waste of time, and that's one of the reasons I don't read "reviews." It's the thing that goes on again and again in reviews, so I don't read them. I'm not interested in coping with poetry. I'm not really interested in dealing with it. I'm mainly interested in getting its vision, getting its energy, getting its vitality, and being inspired by it.

*You mentioned Fresno. You've been a tremendous influence on a lot of very young people. You've shown them that a poem can be written and that it is alive. And yet some of the poets coming out of Fresno have tried very consciously to emulate your poetry. Do you deal with that in any way, or do you just let it run its course?*

Oh no. I tell them to cut it out. I tell them to stop it. There have only been a few. . . . There are a lot of poets who have written a poem that might sound like me, but then they have written eighteen poems like Merwin and twelve like Bly. A lot of poets go through a lot of phases. It's very natural that one be influenced by people close to one. It's an added dimension in the poetry of someone you meet and know and maybe you like the person, but I. . . . So that in the beginning I don't think it's any problem. If a guy's in a freshman class, a very beginning writing class or something, and someone's poetry sounds a little like me, I try not to make too much out of this. If someone's been writing for two or three years and he's really doing my work or anybody else's work too heavily, I try to point that out to him. I try to say, "Well, look. There comes a time when you have to invent your own poetry. You can learn a lot from other people, but I just want you to be conscious of the fact that Bly also wrote a poem about what you're writing, and a better one. And your going into the field and walking up to the horse already took place in a Jim Wright poem, and it's been imitated a thousand times." I think you have a duty to a serious young poet to inform him when you're aware that he's derivative, or overly so, but on the other hand, we do learn by imitating. You've got to be careful about it. You just can't say to everybody, "Don't write like that because somebody else wrote like that," because then I think that one can develop an overly heightened desire to write a new poem, a poem nobody else has written, which can be silly.

*Do you see any particular reasons for the sort of emotional malnutrition that is published as poetry every year, and for the fact that many young poets seem to have one good book of poetry in them and after that it's all downhill? Are they lacking a spiritual or emotional depth in their lives? Are they simply cashing in, bowing out to praise, or what?*

I'm not aware of it, to be honest with you. I don't even know who you could possibly be referring to.

*How about James Tate? Although he has his good poems, individual poems scattered through—*

Yes. But how old is he?

*Maybe thirty-two? Thirty?*

So it seems very presumptuous to say that he's got one good book in him. He may have forty more years of writing life. He's written many good poems, he's been very successful, and because he has been so successful he's probably published everything he writes, whereas with a less successful poet we wouldn't be so aware of his bad poems—they wouldn't be in print.

*That's what I'm getting at. Roethke, for instance, was supposed to have published only about 5 percent of everything he wrote before his death, whereas Tate—I would imagine just from the sheer volume—publishes 90 percent of everything he writes.*

I would tend to think that the late Roethke published a lot more than 5 percent. In the beginning, he had a very hard time making a career of it. And if you'll read his letters, you'll see how much his career meant to him. It's sad to see that he was a careerist in every sense of the word. He worked hard to create his success, and when he got successful he loved it, he ate it up. I don't see anything wrong in liking your success. You would have to be an idiot to be ashamed of your success. I mean, you fail in so many things in life that you might as well get the most out of it. . . . But I'm just not aware of people writing one book and failing. Some people get run over by trains and their lives are cut short, but I'm trying to think of someone who wrote one good book. . . .

*How about Bill Knott or Dennis Schmitz?*

Well, I continue to find the poetry of Schmitz very interesting, and he too is a guy in his early thirties. I didn't publish a book until I was thirty-five years old. I don't know what a book I would have published at twenty-eight would have looked like. It might have looked like shit. The rhythms of people's lives are different. I think, in other words, that you're creating a kind of imaginary villain. The poet who writes one book and "cashes in" as you say, and then turns his back on writing. I don't think it happens. What one frequently finds is that a poet writes the poems of his twenties and in his thirties he's not interested in writing them again. He's not the same guy. In the first place, he's already written those poems and there wouldn't be much sense in writing them again—

*That's one thing—*

Let me finish. The other thing is that he is somebody else. So he begins to write another poem. Maybe he begins to experiment with another style. And if he started early, then of course he's perfected a style. James Tate was awfully good when he was awfully young. A great many American poets weren't even writing at the age that he was very proficient. I was just beginning. So at the age of thirty, he has a lot to throw away before he can find his new style. Maybe it's more difficult for him. I admire the fact that he searches around and tries different things. Also, we tend to think of a poet in a certain way. Knott, for instance. We pick up his first book and say, "Ah, this is just marvelous, terrific." Well, he didn't want to write that book a second time. It was a very wise decision on his part. I don't know whether it was reached in a wise way, but I think he was right. The minute you turn away from doing what you have done already, what people expect of you, even if you do well or ill, you run the risk of blame rather than praise. In spite of what everyone says to the contrary, you're thought of in a certain way. You know, Ginsberg is supposed to write *Howl* again. And I remember when *Kaddish* first came out—I happen to think it's one of the great American poems—but I also happen to know that a great many people were puzzled by it and thought it was a bore.

*OK. Maybe for the sake of conversation I am creating an imaginary villain. But could it be the book publisher's fault also, or publicity?*

Again, I don't think it exists. I think it's your fault. And if this discussion went on in any interesting way, I'd have to ask you why you created this villain. I might ask you now, why do you want these guys to exist? (Laughter) Why do you need to invent them? That's the only fruitful direction we could go. . . .

*I see a lot of talent in a poet like Tate, or Knott, or who-ever, and so much of it seems to be a mindless groping. There are a lot of vacuous spaces. You can read a lot of Tate before you hit upon a good poem. I did a review of his book,* Absences, *and I liked it. It was good, but you have to go through it. There are some awful poems in it, awful.*

Yeah. There are a lot of awful poems in Hardy too, but they don't bother me. You only read them once. Again, it's a question of the way people want to write, and how they write their good poems. If Tate finds that he writes his good poems by writing a lot of poems, then I suppose that's what he has to pursue. If Roethke suppressed 90 percent of his work as you say he did, well, that's the way he worked. Apparently Rilke could sit there for years, with great patience, with the assurance that genuine inspiration would come. I can't, and it would be very foolish of me to assume that I am like Rilke and that I am a great genius, which I'm not, and to sit there and wait for this to happen, because what's going to happen is nothing. I know that. And I don't see any point in judging myself by this other man. I'm a different guy. I have to find the way in which I can write best and pursue it, and encourage other people to find their way, and not belabor them with my way. Again, when you're talking about young people, I think it's premature to talk about their careers. They are really just beginning. I don't know what you would have thought of the work of Wallace Stevens if you could have read it when he was thirty-two. It wasn't even printed until he was in his forties.

*You published your first book,* On The Edge, *when you were thirty-five, and it's a very solid book of poems. You show a lot of talent and craft in it. Your second book,* Not This Pig, *is more relaxed. Overall it's stronger and more varied than* On The Edge. *And then you came out with* They Feed They Lion, *which is a very demanding book to read. It's very aggressive and it's very good. Now you have another book coming out, called* 1933, *which contains poems about your childhood. Is this book more mellow, now that you've gotten that fierceness out in* They Feed They Lion?

I don't think this book is so aggressive. It's very different.

*That doesn't necessarily mean it's weaker, does it?*

No, it doesn't mean it's weaker. It doesn't mean it's stronger either. (Laughter) It just means that it's different. It's a lot less aggressive in that way. There are a lot of poems in it which wouldn't have looked at all out of place in *They Feed They Lion.* In fact, there is a long poem which I considered using in *They Feed They Lion.* It seems very much to be written in the tone and the rhythm of that book, and it's the longest poem in the book. So I don't think there is a clear demarcation.

*If we can assume that you're improving all the time, it ought to be a very strong, powerful book.*

I don't think I am. I don't think I'm getting any better. I may be, but I'm not sure. I don't think about that too much. I think that too is a trap.

*Maybe it's a question you can't answer.*

I don't think it's a question of whether you can answer it or not. If you look back on the careers of poets you'll find that it's a very answerable question. But it's a trap. It's a question that we tend to force on ourselves, when by and large, it's irrelevant to what we're doing. What I'm trying to do is write the poetry of the feelings and experiences I now have. If I don't turn out to be a particularly good poet of middle age, well that's the way it goes. Wordsworth wasn't. He seems middle-aged in his early poems. Curiously enough, he has that wise tone very early in his poetry. You'd think, God, when he got to middle age he'd be. . . . And then we look at Yeats and we see a great poet of middle age. You just do the best you can in any particular period, and I think it's a mistake to look back and say, "Oh shit, I've got to do those poems over again," or "I was better then than I am now." As I said, I think it's a trap that we tend to get ourselves into. I find it's not all that hard to avoid.

*Is it one poem at a time, then?*

No, no. It's not one poem at a time. I get ideas that encompass more than one poem at a time, that almost reach out to the idea of a whole thing I want to write about, like *1933*. Not designs for other poems, but certainly great areas that I want to explore with poetry. This was true with *They Feed They Lion*. I often write on more than one poem at a time.

*You seem to be prolific. Are you?*

Well, it's very different from one occasion to another. Sometimes poems come very quickly, in a great rush, and they're just there. I've written as much as a couple of hundred lines in a day, lines that I've saved and still like a lot. The longest poem I've ever written I wrote in about two days, and it's almost 400 lines. So at times I am very prolific.

*You have* 1933 *coming out in January. And then you're going to Spain in the spring, is that right?*

Europe.

*Is that strictly for writing? Do you have something set, planned that you want to work on over there?*

Oh, it's complicated. It's for a number of reasons.

*OK. Thank you.*

Sure.

# Interview with Stanley Plumly
## and Wayne Dodd

Athens, Ohio, Fall, 1974

*You said last night that you didn't feel you were particularly gifted, and that the poem itself, its coming into being, was a real struggle for you. What did you mean by that?*

Well, I think what I really meant is that, in comparison with some people I have known—friends, and students who became friends—it was clear to me they were able to get places, in terms of writing, with skill and clarity and loveliness, so much faster than I did it, and that they really had a far better ear, for example. I know several who were able to do almost automatically what it took me years to accomplish.

*We live in a time of great technical competence, I think, and facility is what often passes for the real thing. That is obviously not what is in your work. It's something else happening, something much more real, deeper.*

You have to really work very hard to get a poem right. And once you get a sense that you got it the way you want it—and you've gone through a hell of a hard time doing it—well, there's such an incredible sense of achievement. Some of my friends, who were terrifically gifted, ultimately didn't do anything, and I wonder if maybe having it come so easily, they didn't value it as much as they might have. And then when they changed, when they got older, that kind of writing no longer seemed interesting. . . . It seemed terrific for someone in his late teens, but it didn't seem like much for someone in his middle thirties. They didn't even like it themselves.

*Maybe it was what they were writing about. So many things that offer themselves up to facility aren't worth worrying about.*

Well, you know, in a way they never wrote about a hell of a lot, the people I'm talking about. They never wrote about anything. They wrote about the surfaces of their poems. My poems wouldn't be worth a damn if they were just the surfaces of the poems, and they obviously looked like shit when they were. Which in a way is an advantage. I mean, these other guys can write rings around you if you're going to use your little Wallace Stevens typewriter. You just say forget it, I'll go someplace else, it wasn't what I wanted to do anyway.

꩜

*How long have you lived in California?*

I came here in '57.

*Do you long to go back and drink motor oil in Detroit?*

No, I don't. I've only been back to Detroit once since '68. I read there in '68 and I wasn't treated very well by a number of people, and I was made aware of certain facts. People invest you, I think, with emotions that they don't know what to do with. You are somebody who was part of their life at one time. They think you've gone on to become a movie star, or some goddamn thing. Some people go one way, some people go another way. I get letters from people I went to high school with that are just wonderful, you know. Or guys I knew at college, and women. I get a letter about every year or so, saying, "Gee, it's terrific that you really stuck it out, you stayed and you really did become a poet." But when I go home, I see a lot of other people that don't feel that way at all. They want to shoot me down, and I had just a miserable time with people that I had felt were very close to me. I suppose they were close to me; if they hadn't been close to me, they wouldn't have had to be shitty to me. Well then, when I went back this spring, I went by myself. I went to downtown Detroit and walked around for a day, or half a day. Then I went back to Ann Arbor to read and got stuck in a traffic jam because a garbage truck had overturned, and it seemed like an absolutely appropriate "Welcome Home, Levine!" But I bumped into a couple of people downtown, and they were wonderful to me. One guy said to me, a guy that I knew from a gym, an immense gorilla of a guy, and a very handsome guy, and I hadn't seen him since he was about twenty and I was probably about twenty-two. I recognized him instantly, but I couldn't think of his name. I was coming out of an elevator, and we just stared at each other, and then he said to me, "Bill Ghesquiere." Which was his name. "Yaco's Gym." Which is where he knew he knew me. And I said, "Phil Levine." He said, "Yeah, of course." And then he recalled that he had once showed me some poetry of his. He was, you know, this huge physical specimen. He was Mr. Michigan, he was a weight lifter, and all this. He was a secret poet. He said, "Yeah, I showed you poetry once, remember?" "Yes," I said, "sure." He said, "What did you ever do, did you ever stay in that poetry thing?" I said, "Oh yeah, I'm a poet." "You are?" he said. And I said, "What are you? What did you do?" He said, "I'm an a . . . a lawyer." He was going to say attorney, but he said lawyer. And then I said . . . you know, we were just standing there, like two dummies, and I said to him—it was really a stupid question—I said, "How's it been?" The guy's life is now two-thirds up, and he gave me the most incredible answer, not verbally, but mainly just with his face. About nine different emotions passed over his face, you know. There was a moment of just utter collapse, and then a smile, a little wry smile, and finally the smile came back and remained and he said, "OK." It was really lovely.

*Like a man drowning in his whole past.*

Yes, it starts bubbling up—"How's it been?" You haven't seen him for twenty-five years, and you'll never see him again. Then he said, "We'll have to get together sometime." And he walked away. Of course I had no idea of how to get together with him. Or he with me.

*Your talking about that event in your past reminds me of what keeps stirring my mind as I read and think about your poetry: namely, the crucial importance, the sense of the continuity of life to your poems, the recapitulation, your going back and picking it up, going back and looking at the past, looking at things that happened to you, getting these little things in, and finding out what they mean—and trying to get some sense out of it. So I wondered—take two very obvious poems that are dealing with the same subject: your earlier poem, "Coming Homeward from Toledo," and the more recent poem, "1933." These are both talking essentially about the same thing, or trying to deal with the same thing very differently. But what do you think is the different dimension involved in the later poem? Does that seem to you a sensible question?*

Yes, but I don't think I can answer it, because I'm really not aware of what the different dimension is. Maybe there's less that would trouble me reading some of the more recent than some of the older poems. Maybe I like them better. I don't really know why I like them better. I think they're quite different. I have the feeling that if you took that one poem and stuck it in the other book, it wouldn't look right. It would look kind of . . . I'm not that conscious of what I'm doing, and I have very few theories—I don't know if I have any—about poetry. I have a lot of beliefs in what it does and why it's useful to have it, to be in contact with it, and I know that I have to write it. But I'm not really that conscious of my own poetry and I'm not sure I want to be.

I know I have certain obsessions, and I think one of them comes out of the impermanence of growing up in a modern city where nothing remains very long what it was. I learn a lot through seeing how other people live. I see my wife's incredibly powerful relationship with landscape, with animals, with trees, things like that, as a rural person. I know that I have a corresponding relationship with buildings and street corners, places and streets that I've known. In a way, you have the feeling that the spirit of the oak tree is in almost any oak tree. It's not true about street corners: somehow they have a quality—it's a Polish street corner—but it isn't anymore. You go back, and it's all gone. Even by the time I had finished high school, much of the past had disappeared, it was gone. The streets were torn down, something else was put there. Or the neighborhood was changed by the moving out of one ethnic group and the moving in of another. It was an incredibly unstable kind of thing, and one which horrified me.

I remember when my grandfather died—I must have been about twenty-five—it seemed that this immense link with the past was gone. I could talk with him about Russia; I could talk to him about what *we* were. My grandmother, I didn't talk about things like that with. And she wouldn't have answered. She was crazy to be an American. She was in earnest about being an American, although I think she was fooling only herself. There was a poem . . . I'm afraid I don't remember the name of it, but I published a poem back in maybe '55 or so about my grandfather and his last days. It's probably a very inexpert poem; I think it's probably kind of clumsy, but in some ways very much like my later poetry. It's full of things, objects, scenes. He does play cards with me in the poem, I remember that. There are some similarities. It's a very different poem. It's a straight narrative. I'm taking care of him in a cabin outside the city. He's been sick, and I'm sort of nursing him. We're on this lake, and he's a bit bored, too. We go out and fish, and he's not into that shit. I mean, he's supposed to be recovering from illness, but he's bored. He wants the action of the city and all that. We play cards. But what I'm immensely conscious of is how everything's going, going—vanishing. And I heard that in the poem I read last night to my mother, the same obsession with my boy becoming a man, too fast. Eating everything, eating it up. It's probably a contemporary urban awareness or a terror that you have if you come out of the situation. When I go home, I'm lost. I'm lost in Detroit. There are all those freeways I never . . . I can't find my way around. This spring we went back to Spain, went back to the village in which we had lived, which had been tiny, and we got lost. It had grown so much we actually didn't know where we were.

*So telling stories about these places is a way of slowing or impeding that disappearance? Because you do, relentlessly, tell stories about it, right? Would you say that the greatest impulse in your poetry is narrative?*

No, no I don't think that. I don't feel about it as an impulse. It's what I like to do. I love to write little narratives. Bob Mezey was reading all my new poems this spring when I went to read at Missoula, and he was just sitting there reading and he looked up and said, "You're a storyteller. You're a storyteller." He's only known me twenty years, and he finally saw it.

*Well, he's right in a sense. It's even more profoundly true in the new poems, since the 1933 poems.*

Well, I think if you go back to *Not This Pig*, it's very true there. My favorite poems are poems like "Heaven," the one about the guy with the bird; and "The Midget" is just a story. I did write short stories.

I did write novels. I began writing as a poet, but I put it aside very quickly. I wanted to be a fiction writer, and worked as a fiction writer for several years. I realized after a while my temperament was all wrong for it. My impatience.

*We talked a moment ago about the facility of some poets, and felicity of some poets. But your poems always seem so uneasy in their harness; that struggle is always so apparent, and I think that is one of the great powers and virtues of your work. As if it's about to burst out and be something else. I don't know what. Maybe a story or something indeterminate. Maybe that's why you're not a theoretician about your work; you don't think about it like that, but the nature of the form is always calling itself into question as the poem is being made on the page.*

Well, I took classes in New Criticism and that kind of crap because my teachers had been trained in that. That was enough for me. I didn't like what we finally wound up with as a reading of a poem, and I didn't like it as a *way* of reading. It didn't do anything for me. I could play chinese checkers and figure out chess problems. . . . It seemed to me that there was a kind of deadness in the way we were dealing with the stuff, and that if you were to say suddenly to the teacher, "This goddamn poem doesn't seem very spontaneous. It isn't very exciting," he'd look at you like "spontaneous" and "exciting" were terrible words.

*All premeditation.*

Yes, "What's that got to do with? *Spontaneous?* That's what you *say*." I remember Yvor Winters, who was my teacher: "Poetry shouldn't be like speech. Speech is fragmentary, blurred. Poetry is forever, and chiseled."

*Winters was a teacher of yours?*

That's an odd word. He was an acquaintance. Actually, I got along with him very well until the subject turned to poetry. It almost never did. We almost never talked about poetry. In the end, I found— well the first thing was, I liked his wife; I thought she was a wonderful, wonderful person. And through Winters, my wife and I met a marvelous person who became a lifelong friend, an older woman. And he was kind to me, he was a kind man, in a lot of ways. He was terribly clumsy. He wanted to be kind, and he didn't quite know how. In the classroom he was disaster. He read from his essays. He read *In Defense of Reason* in one course. And the students sat there. He was very unperceptive on the level of relationships with people, incredibly. He was obviously a very close, brilliant reader of poetry. Even when you didn't agree with his evaluation of a poem, it was clear he could read it very carefully. But it was pathetic the way the students suckered him, kissed his ass, and those were the ones he liked. Kids who had some gumption . . . he wanted to like but didn't. They were "Mad. Mad." You know, he overused the word "mad." Oh, he was sad. He was a frustrated prizefighter—underneath all that "right reason"—and he hadn't the vaguest idea how to box. He would show me how he would fight, and I would say to him (I also trained for a couple of years to fight; I was no good . . . I mean, even though I could have beaten

Yvor Winters with my head), it was sad to see that under all this mind business was a man with an unhappy body.

*One of the things I like about* 1933: *that tone shifted to the deeper well of the past. A great deal more love came out of whatever happened on the page.*

It goes much farther back. There isn't anything in *They Feed They Lion* that really goes back farther than young manhood. In *1933* I go all the way back to myself as a tiny boy about four. My father died when I was five, and some of those scenes there are when I'm three or four.

*I find* They Feed They Lion *a very different book.*

It is, yes. A lot of people didn't like it. That's been the history of my writing, of people's response to it. I think that's probably the history of everybody's writing. If you write a book and people like it, they want you to do it all over again. And that's why I couldn't sell *They Feed They Lion.* I mean, it just sat there for years, three or four years, being soundly rejected. And always, "We liked your last book. It was so nice, why did you stop doing that?"

*Why is* 1933 *the title of the new book?*

It seems to me it's the title because the act, the deprivation, the shock that occurs when the world takes the father away is the central concern of the book. It becomes an act that reaches deep as it can into the kid. In the first poem, there is a question—"Where did my father go?"—and that's the question of the book, really: "Where did he go?"

⁊

*You know, it strikes me that one of the things that sets you apart from your contemporaries is that most American poets, of your time, especially, tend to be country poets. And there are some suburban poets. John Hollander is, I think, a suburban poet. I think Anthony Hecht is, finally, a suburban poet. But you are a city poet. You are an urban poet. I can't think of anyone else who comes close to you in evoking that sense of . . . it's not exactly nostalgia, but of finding that way back, and epiphanizing it.*

I know such profound differences, for example, between my wife and me, in the way that we relate to the same people, say. I'm a very defensive person. Less so as the years go on. And that's in the poems, too.

*Sure, you're a boxer, you've got that left hand up.*

Yes, that's right. And I've learned what I think are hard things about people, because I've seen people at their worst. And if you've seen people at their worst, in bad times . . . you know, you work with people and you like them a lot, but you also know that you don't leave your wallet in your pants when you hang them up, because you shouldn't tempt people who haven't got anything. Because they're going to take it, goddamn it. As you would. So there are hard things you know about people if you've seen them in an urban situation where everybody was up against it. And you learn that the first thing is, you defend yourself. If you don't defend yourself, either you are destroyed or you make other people defend you, which is not a very manly or womanly thing to do, because when they defend you, then they have to stop defending themselves. You cost your friends too much. Your friends can't always be defending you: they've got to defend themselves. Many years ago I got into an occurrence that appears in one of the poems. It's the root of "Silent in America," and it also appears in the poem "Thistles," where I'm in a fight, and I get beat up. And I remember my wife's attitude toward it and mine were so different. My attitude was that I got exactly what I had coming. I knew better. What had happened was, a beloved big-mouth friend of mine helped this fight to take place. It didn't have to happen. I mean, there were these two guys, one of them was a wrestler, a university jock-wrestler, and the other was a football player. And they were immense by comparison to me and my dwarf friend. He talked to them in a way I never talk to people that size. You took one look at them and you knew they were ready to kill you for the slightest excuse. So if you've got wits, goddamnit, use them. Well, he called one a mother-fucker. Well, the guy knocked him down and just began to kick him. I intervened at that point. People thought, my wife thought of me as being so brave and foolhardy. I thought of myself as being an asshole. I said to her, "Not only did he ask for the beating, he needed it." He needed it, right then and there. He didn't need to get killed . . . the guy wasn't going to kill him . . . he might have knocked some teeth out or something. But the guy wound up breaking *my* jaw, kicking *me* in the mouth. But my friend needed it, not me. Because I would never say that to an ape. And as the years went on, my wife saw that I was right. He did need that, because he went on to make similar mistakes. If he had learned it at that age, in his twenties, his whole life might have been a lot better, I think. Even if he had three or four teeth missing. He went on to make other mistakes like that, to put other people in situations like that. He wised up finally, but it took another ten or twelve years. It cost him a lot. He'd have been better off to have gotten the shit beat out of him. I didn't need it at all. I had already had the shit beat out of me . . . many, many times. That kind of stance is also in the poetry, in many of the poems. I don't much like it, to tell the truth. I don't like to be that way. I don't feel that way all the time now. By no means.

*Those are the poems that work least well for me, too. That's why I think* 1933 *is your finest book.*

I don't agree. I like *They Lion* better. I think if you go back . . . well, some of the poems in my first book are really hurt by that stance. But I haven't lived in the city in a long time. I realize, when I go to the city now, that in many ways I'm not equipped for it. My guard *is* down.

*There's a resounding* no *in some of your poems. They don't agree, of course, with anything. They disagree with everything.*

I don't feel that way about them. I really believe my

poems are a resounding *yes*. That's the way I read them. But they're very contradictory. I forget that. There's a lot of contradiction.

*Basically, they are affirmative, I agree. But they are affirming against a lot of things.*

I've surprised myself with all the anger in my recent writing. I had thought I wasn't quite so angry any more.

*This is not really social anger, though it's anger against societally imposed attacks. It's not aggressions against individuals. It's a very personal thing. You're not, in the sense that a Kenneth Patchen was, and often very badly so, a didactic poet . . .*

He was also just a fantastically good poet at times. Jesus, fabulous. Beautiful poet. I wish I'd found him earlier. But you know, I was shown his bad poems . . . which were kind of popular when I was young. A lot of his lousy, sort of "cute" poems were well liked, and the best poems were almost unknown. I didn't find them until *Naked Poetry*—well almost then. In England, just before *Naked Poetry* came out, I bought Patchen's *Selected Poems* that an Englishman had done. I thought, Jesus Christ, the English, not one of whom has ever written anything like this . . . they can appreciate him, we bury him. I felt terrific kinship with him.

*Well, I'm glad I brought him up, because I felt that too, and I wasn't sure how you'd feel about that parallel. But there is a kind of tyranny that you're objecting to. I don't know if it's a tyranny of the mind, or what it is. But there's so much will in your work. I can't think of another poet who has so much sheer power of will. As you say, going against whatever. And I wish I could find that thing you're going against. It isn't sociological, strictly speaking. You're not protesting the war in Vietnam or urban conditions or any such thing. It's personal, it's deeper than that.*

I think a lot of it comes from the time of someone precisely my age in America discovering, when they're quite young—fourteen or fifteen or something—an immense lie. Your whole notion of reality was a lie, it was just a lie. Your country wasn't what you had been told it was, the others weren't what you'd been told they were. Nobody was what you'd been told they were. The past was utter horseshit. The constitution was not the beautiful document; nobody ever listened to it anyway, and the guys who wrote it had slaves. This sudden, just fantastic shock—and then it went on and on—it went on through the forties and into the fifties. Our great allies in the movies, the Russians, overnight became some fiendish devils. Such a bizarre world you lived in. There were so many lies within lies.

*I don't know how you go over in translation (of course it would depend upon the language), but you would seem to me to be a very popular poet in Europe. The way Patchen was. Patchen was much more popular in Europe in his own lifetime than he was in this country. Much more well known. He was the popular American poet of his time. In Europe.*

Is that right? Maybe I need to go over there. Get a little recognition.

*But it seems to me you've brought your heritage with you from Russia, your Jewish heritage from Russia. When you say "the state," you identify the state as the aggressor, and that seems to me unusual.*

Unusual? The state *is* the enemy. There's a little thing that occurs in one of my poems called "Saturday Sweeping." It's a poem that takes place during the Korean War. The "I" in the poem, the "me," is looking forward to what's going to come in Detroit. He's alone, he's got this apartment, he's sweeping it out. He talks about the isolation of each life in this little apartment. He says "If anybody knocks on your door, it will be this, it will be that, it will be the great talking dogs that saved the Jews." Well, that was a little story I was told as a child. My grandfather would put me to bed with little tales. One of them was about a talking dog who would be privy to the secrets of the mad Russian murderers, and then come and warn the Jews. And I found this a very engaging story, but then as I got older I realized the cynicism of it, that if you were going to get any help, you'd have to get it from animals. Because people weren't going to do shit for you. You'd more likely get it from a talking dog. He had a great storyteller's ability to mask, to hide the meaning until you could handle it. As a boy, I found this story charming.

◦➣◦

*This is going to wrench things around quite a bit, but to shift into another gear: when you look around you in American poetry today, what do you see? What do you like, what do you not like?*

I don't really know. It doesn't seem to me that things

look as good as they did five, six, seven years ago. I remember when the book *Naked Poetry* came out, it seemed to me very exciting that there were a bunch of poets, roughly in their late thirties or early forties, who were writing—there were a number of different styles—and they were handling poems with a lot of authority, with a lot of real subject matter. I'm not sure that most of the poets in the book have gone on to do as well as we'd already done—without naming anybody in particular, which I don't like to do. I don't know the explanation to that. People mark time. They write bad books, and you say "That's terrible, cut it out." I don't do that, I don't say that's a terrible book. I don't know what some other poet . . . what his rhythm is. Maybe he or she has to just do nothing, or do something bad. I've written a lot of bad stuff. The difference between me and some of the other poets is that, coming late to acceptance, I didn't publish most of my worst stuff. I couldn't even publish my good stuff, much less my worst stuff. So I had to sit with it a long time. So that so much of my bad work has disappeared. I've thrown it away. Somebody who got known much earlier, in their twenties, all their poems are available. I don't know whether they know, as well as I know, that people who finally pat you on the head don't know their ass from a hole in the ground. So that if you make the mistake of believing that you're as good as some people will tell you—as anybody tells you—if you don't finally, for yourself, determine where you are, you can really trick yourself. I'm afraid that some of us may have done that.

*They have believed their press?*

Maybe. And maybe they have created their press, too. I remember first seeing a writer like Louis Simpson in a little essay use the word "great" in speaking of Wright and Bly as "great poets." This is maybe ten years ago, someplace, in some review or something—and I thought to myself, "Well, that's an odd word, I don't know if *Keats* is a great poet. What the hell is this character talking about?" And Louis Simpson is a bright guy, and he's a very good poet. But what good can come from saying "He's great"?

All right, there was a kind of immediate good. Everybody sort of got up on their hind legs and said, "Well, we don't have to feel like shits just because of Stevens and Williams and all those big guys. We're pretty good, too." That was a good thing, it seemed to me. But then there was that other thing: "Well, then if I'm a great poet, I guess I can just about start collecting my correspondence." I don't think Wright and Bly did that, but it must have been harder for them after hearing that again and again. I think it's a real mistake. I mean, my own feeling about my work is very different. I think I'm a good poet—I don't know who's better than anybody else, frankly. I think that there are a lot of good people writing, but I think that my attitude is probably very different from some people who got discovered in their twenties instead of their forties. My attitude is, if I die tomorrow, I'll be forgotten the day after. There will be a little black-bordered square in *Poetry* magazine: "Philip Levine." And then my poor wife will have to bring out a posthumous volume which will languish on book shelves, and then that's it. I really don't think it's going to change anything, I just don't think it's good enough to last. I don't know what is.

*Are you hopeful that, if you don't die tomorrow, you're going to come around to writing stuff that is good and enduring?*

I've always believed that with some luck, a good deal of luck, and hard work, I could write a poetry that would . . . I'm not ashamed of what I've done; in fact I'm kind of proud of it. In a curious way, I've already written better than I thought I would. I never thought I would write as well as I have written. I had a weird, irrational belief that there was entrusted to me, you know, just an enormous thing that had to be said. I was the guy who had to say it, nobody else could say it. That's all there was to it. If I didn't write it, it wasn't going to get written. I might not write it, but I had to try. I haven't actually written a lot of poetry that I was supposed to write. So there's still a lot of work to be done. I feel there is a lot of work to be done. Americans have never really handled that thing of early success well. It's a cliché, but it's gotten to so many writers of fiction, poets too. And maybe there's an advantage in coming from a place like Detroit where there isn't an option, the way I've seen it done, to bargain for a kind of success, to play those games. I went to Fresno, and in a way, I just lived in the boondocks. I don't mean to say that it didn't hurt me to be unknown, it did. It was painful: to pick up the fucking magazines and this guy gets a Guggenheim and he can't write at all; and I've got to work at this shitty job. That's what hurt. Time. I was getting screwed out of the time I had coming. But I also realized that in order to get that time, this guy spent almost as much time as he got earning points or I don't know what. He lived a life I couldn't find bearable, or so I said to myself, so I sort of petted myself with that. I said, "It's all right, you've got it just as well; their lives are hateful, too." Of course I didn't know, I never will know what their lives were like. Galway was the guy whose career, in many ways, was a lot like mine. He didn't publish a book until he was thirty-five or so.

*But he's also a poet who has struggled a great deal with the very sense of making a line.*

You look at those early poems, oh God. All those lines are saying to him, "Don't write like this, don't write like this." Except for a few poems.

*That's an interesting parallel, but for another reason. There is no imputation of influence or anything of that sort in this question. But I do think that you and Galway share something in the kind of line and rhetorical sweep of your poetry that you don't share with a lot of your contemporaries right now. In other words, you're mining the same vein, or the influence is coming from a similar place, or you're hearing the same kinds of rhythms and music. There is, it seems to me, an enormous rhetorical sweep to your poetry. But it's not rhetorical poetry at all. A great on-rushing energy, as there is to Galway's.*

I admire Galway's poetry enormously. He does things that I don't do, and don't try to do. He has a sense of the voluptuousness of language, which is a way in which he enriches his poems enormously. I can't do that, I mean, I just can't. I don't even re-member if I tried. I must have tried it. I've tried everything at one time or another, probably before I'd read Galway, because I didn't become aware of

Galway until other people did also—until after the one poem in the first book, *What a Kingdom It Was,* "The Avenue Bearing the Initial of Christ into the New World." And then the second book I didn't like as well, really. I was let down. But it was a different kind. And then *Body Rags* just seemed to be a blazing kind of book. It had some incredible poems in it. And I love *The Book of Nightmares,* although I find a lot of people won't forgive its bad writing.

*There is some bad writing in it.*

Big fucking deal. Do they realize that most books are mostly bad writing? When it's good, it's so incredible! And I like the way he takes chances. I suppose he's probably my favorite poet of my contemporaries. Early Ginsberg I thought was incredible. *Howl.* And *Kaddish* I thought was just an incredible poem in another way. Never had the language that Galway had. It seems to me that recently Ginsberg's . . . I don't know . . . I don't see how anyone can live Ginsberg's life and write poetry, and from talking with him, I gather that he doesn't either, and he wishes people would go away and leave him alone.

e❧o

*There is to me a sense of sweat, a sense of earned effort in your poetry—not that this effort shows, but it is clearly the source of much of the passion in your work—especially* 1933.

You know, that was the thing, as a young man, that kept me alive, in a way. I remember working in a factory where we made engine blocks for Cadillacs, and one day a whole bunch of very well-dressed people came through, and they were being shown around, I don't know if it was their daddy's factory or what, and they were looking at us, you know, and I could have picked up, if I'd had the strength, one of those blocks and killed them with it. And then I worked on construction crews a lot, too, building roads and stuff. I was aware of the fact—also I was a truck driver—that you would go to places where people would be dressed up, you would be delivering. I worked for railroad express. I remember going in the autumn to Grosse Pointe and getting the trunks marked "Vassar," "Harvard," "Yale," what have you. I had a sense that what I had. . . . All right, their lives had a jump on mine, in a lot of ways. Mine had the jump on theirs in a number of ways. One of them was that I worked, that I could do it. When the pestilence came, and the maid didn't answer the buzzer, they'd die, those fuckers. But I could go on living. There's a way in which I prided myself. I mean, I had to find some way to say, "Well, it isn't altogether hopeless." And I think one of the things that sustained me was that I could do this work. I could live in the shittiest goddamn circumstances. If I could only not eat myself up with bitterness, I could be OK. That was the one real worry. I was aware of that, too. You could devour yourself from the inside out. With bitterness for the inequity of it all, and their lack of concern. It isn't so bad that it's unequal, it's that you have to *see* that it's unequal, and they're laughing. For all the wrong reasons. So work is something I . . . yes, I like to work. That's another thing, I like to write poetry, I like to work. Sometimes I hate it, but ultimately, I like it.

*But do you see it as work?*

Yes, I see it as work. But as I say, I like to work. I hate it, but I like it. I love the sense of feeling used afterwards. I've been used. To me, the worst fucking thing in the world is to pass from this place unused . . . I have a major in a poem on an airplane in *Not This Pig*, where I talk about his eyes being light blue and unused. My heroes are all used. Not *mis*used. I don't want to be misused, the way we so often misuse a person: use him against his will, use him for things that aren't good for him. But I want to use myself, and I want to use other people well. We're self-conscious about being used. "I'm being used." Well, what the fuck are you going to do, just sit home all day? "Nobody's using me . . . and I'll be damned if I'll be my worst enemy and use myself."

*Are you aware of any difference in the work you're doing right now, here in the wake of 1933, as opposed to the growth from* They Feed They Lion *to* 1933, *and so forth?*

Oh yes, the poems have surprised me. Really. I took a couple months off, and prayed they just wouldn't come out the same. I waited, and they did come out differently, and I was very thankful. I'm aware of the fact that they're different. They're cleaner, I think, in terms of the way they move.

*They're easier to read, for one thing. They're more generous. They're more relaxed. Their emotions are more generous, too, and I think they're more embracing.*

Not all of them; you haven't seen them all. Some of them are furious. They're really angry. And sardonic.

*What about the length of the line. There are lots of poems in* 1933, *for example, with short lines, with clipped lines.*

There are a lot of short-line poems that I'm writing now, but the movement is different. They're much more lyrical. The movement from line to line seems to me more relaxed and softer. Again, with long sentences. But more flowing, I think. I've written a lot of poetry since *1933,* certainly, that I like as much . . . I mean, I now have enough to put together and make a book as long as *1933,* maybe longer. I don't quite see how I'm going to put it all together, though. I'm in no hurry.

*The stuff I've seen seems to be terribly domestic in the sense that you've gone, even more, to your own family past, and your family present. You're using a lot of incidentals right out of your . . .*

Then there are some other poems not. There are some larger poems. I mean in terms of their scope. But then there are a lot of the poems of the past.

*Is your wife a critic of your poems for you, I mean a sounding board?*

Well, given the fact that she speaks in a code, she's my best critic. I have to interpret the code. I forced her to use it. I get what I got coming. She begins with just slightly under "immortal," and ends with "ineffable," and "incandescent"; and that means, that runs from shit to OK when you translate it. Yes, she's a very sharp critic, I think she has missed some poems, everybody misses some. Now, my next best critic is my friend Peter Everwine. The first time I showed him "To P. L.," he said, "Boring." Fran said, "Fantastic." He said, "Boring." And I thought, well, what do you do? I looked around for a tie-breaker. Actually, finally, I think my friends are helpful on local things, but . . . Everwine has a wonderful ear, and he asks wonderful questions about poems, like "Why did you say this?" He's very gentle and when you look at it you see that you shouldn't have, or whatever. There were guys in the past who were very helpful, who were readers, but who don't really, for one reason or another, give me much help any more. I think as you grow older or you get better known, it's probably harder to get real criticism, so that means now I do use my wife as a critic more than I did ten years ago. Anybody would tell me, "That stinks," ten years ago. But now, "God, I better not tell him that stinks. God, I might need a favor." I don't know, I mean I don't know what's operating. There's also another thing. They have a hesitancy. . . . That was unfair. It was ungenerous, and I don't think it's true. It isn't that they need a favor from me. It's that now they're very uncertain of their judgments about my poems, because they've made judgments about poems in the past and then seen that I had taken a change in my work and they didn't see it coming, and they didn't like it at first, and now they think they were wrong. Like Bob Mezey, who mostly is a brilliant critic of my work: he also disliked some of my best poems, shortly after I wrote them. And then a year later he'd hear me read one and he'd say, "Gee, that's a wonderful poem." And I'd say, "What are you talking about? You said it was a big turkey the last time." He'd say, "Oh no, you must be thinking of someone else." And I'd dig out of a drawer a copy with his comment, "That stinks. This stinks. Save a few lines, you've got nothing here." So having known that to happen, I think he's gotten a bit hesitant to be wrong again. I wish he'd be wrong again, frankly. I don't mind people reading my poems and . . . I want harsh, honest criticism. I've finally got to evaluate. I never defend my own poems. Even when people are tough on your poems, they often tell you very useful things about them that you haven't told yourself. And they should. But of course I also want praise. It's hard for my friends—they've got to be honest *and* praise the poem.

*Are you writing more now than you ever have? You got a Guggenheim this year, right?*

Oh, this has been a terrific year. But I started writing a lot more in 1965 than I had ever written before. Let's see how old I would have been . . . thirty-seven. That was the first year I went to Spain and didn't work at a job. Somehow I began to write more, and I've written a lot more ever since then. This is probably one of my best years, though, because I'm not teaching. I didn't teach then either. And then the next time I went back to Spain, in 1968, I wrote an enormous amount. Got sick, though. I had some bad years after that, just within my head. But I wrote a lot. Unrest doesn't seem to . . . doesn't seem to stop me. So far, anyway. I also believe, I'm sort of . . . you shouldn't crow . . . you shouldn't think you're going to go on just because the past looks glorious. I've already, like I suppose anybody my age, I've already done things I said I'd never do, that I didn't look upon as things that human beings ought to do. You know, I've made discoveries about myself that were very unpleasant. I condemned other people that didn't seem to me worked as hard, without sympathy for the fact that they probably were trying as best they could.

*You seem in turmoil almost all the time. By turmoil, I mean you're constantly reevaluating things. Nothing is set. Maybe that's in fact what you're missing in those old criticisms from some people. You want more of that turmoil, you want more of that tension.*

Maybe.

*Some people just sit on their anxieties.*

Yes, when I finish a poem, I finish it because I can't do any more work on it. Not because it's in bronze. I had a friend tell me he'd never rewrite. Once the imagination has committed itself to the page, who would he be to interfere with it. He's carrying around this little piece of God in him. Well, I'm carrying around a little piece of God in me, too—I think we all are—but if I speak, I speak through my very human and cocky cracked voice. If you don't use your brains now and then, you're just a fucking dummy. I'm not into automatic writing. Although a lot of the stuff comes through very swiftly, you know. I don't think any of it would have come if I hadn't worked my ass off, though.

*Why did you start writing more in 1969? Simply because for the first time in a long time you had some time off and didn't have other things to do?*

I think that was a major reason. And then, I needed the writing. I needed to be working. I think up until 1969 my poetry had almost always, in a way, been there when I needed it. In the sense of needing it psychologically. I needed to be making poems. It was what I had been hanging on to. In 1969 it was the first time I was both able to write and not be helped by it, to write well and still feel the need of something else. Maybe a pill. It was probably what . . . I don't know myself, now . . . it was probably what so many people go through entering middle age. It makes all our friends bananas for a while. I'm willing to live with a lot of ignorance. It was a shock, though, to discover that you could both write and sink. Not hurt so much as sink. But as you were going under, you were writing quite well. Weird.

*Yes, good poems don't necessarily make your life any better. They may make it a lot worse.*

The other day I was sitting on the train with a young woman, going from Syracuse to Poughkeepsie to give a reading, and she was studying mime. No, we were going from Poughkeepsie to New York City . . . and she began talking about mime and what you had to learn first. It was amazing how much it was like poetry. She would talk about these problems she would work on, and it was all very vague at first, so I said to her, "Well, what the hell is a real problem, tell me one." She said, "Well, like looking someone in the eyes." It was sort of startling. "In all our movements and everything we're taught a kind of sense of defense. But mime is a condition of vulnerability." So much of being a poet is looking other people in the eyes. Looking yourself in the eyes. And accepting your vulnerability. Which is a very hard lesson for me, to accept the fact that if I were really going to write well, I'd have to take certain kinds of risks. Emotional risks. And I didn't really know what they were, what they were going to entail. You bring out the past, you know.

*You suffer those original losses, and in reenacting you make those poems about losses, and then that's another loss.*

You just don't know what's going to happen. You know what will happen if you don't deal with them. Nothing. But then I don't know what will happen if they come up. Because they actually come up. I don't so nearly search for my poems as they find me. I don't run away from them. Which is what I see some people do. I mean, there's no way the poem is going to find you if you're playing ping-pong. Or cha-cha-cha-ing. Chasing girls, or whatever it is you chase. Perfecting your back stroke. I mean, there's no way. You have to be there. In some state of readiness and hospitality to the fucking muse, you know, who is, after all, only a part of you. You have to let it open the door and come into your brain, into your hand, wherever it comes. And I do a lot of that. I mean I sit lots of hours picking my nose. I don't even pick my nose. I do nothing. I've learned that you have to do nothing. You have to be silent and see if the voice will enter you.

# Interview with Studs Terkel

Chicago, Illinois, Spring, 1977

*In this highly industrial age, in this postindustrial age, you might say, there are poets still around and about the country. Of course we know of the more celebrated ones, naturally, but there are some who should be far better known than they are, excellent ones. Philip Levine is a good example, and Robert Mazzocco in a long review in the* New York Review of Books *wrote, "Over the last few years Philip Levine has become so striking a poet that I'm surprised he's not more highly valued than he is. . . . He can create the sense of a milieu, the sound, feel, geography of a place, a time, a people, the flavor of what's been happening among us and what continues, which seems to me almost totally lacking in most other serious poetry today." And so my guest is Philip Levine. By the way, you'll hear his voice and his poetry on one of the Caedmon records. In a moment some of the readings and reflections of poet Philip Levine.*

[Philip Levine reads "Grandmother in Heaven."]

### Grandmother in Heaven

Darkness gathering in the branches
of the elm, the car lights going home,

someone's beautiful Polish daughter
with a worn basket of spotted eggs,

an elbow of cabbage, carrots, leaves,
chicken claws scratching the air,

she comes up the cracked walk to the stairway
of shadows and lost dolls and lost breath.

Beautiful Polish daughter with hands
as round and white as buns, daughter

of no lights in the kitchen, no one sits
on the sofa, no one dreams in the tub,

she in her empty room in heaven
unpacking the basket piece by piece

on the silent, enamelled table
with a little word for each, a curse

for the bad back and the black radish
and three quick spits for the pot.

*And so this poem about your grandmother, beginning way
way back in memory, as Grace Shulman, who is the poetry
editor of the* Nation, *spoke of your remarkable way with
commonplace detail: the radish, the bun, the spit in the fire.
You the poet, how it came to be, how you came to be, Philip
Levine?*

Yeah, I think that urge to memorialize details is part
of my urban inheritance. Growing up I saw whole
neighborhoods disappear, change their character.

*This is Detroit?*

Yes. People move away, new people move in, buildings torn down. Now when I go back home I'm invariably a stranger. I get lost very quickly. There are freeways where there used to be houses that I lived in, and places that had a lot of meaning for me are simply gone. One of the earliest motives in my writing is in a way in response to that. It was an effort to slow down this voracious eating of time of everything that I cared for. I hope to preserve some image, a verbal image. I didn't have the power to preserve any other kind of image.

*So the image is also a landmark, a landmark of something that was but no longer is.*

Yes. These people were here and they meant something. They did something, and nobody remembers them, and I see one of my central functions as the person who remembers them and records their qualities.

*Is it right to describe you as a city poet? A poet of the city?*

A lot of my reviewers have said that, and people who have written about me have said that. It probably distinguishes me from almost all the other poets writing in the country today. So many of them are concerned with the rural and ecology. Then there are a lot of what people call "suburban" poets. I'm really one of the few after Kenneth Patchen, who was a real urban poet too and an inspiration to me, to really center his work around the city, to love the city. It's kind of popular to think of the city as antinatural, antihuman, destructive. I happen to be married to a rural woman, and she's taught me a profound respect for animals, trees, flowers, things growing, that I didn't have because I didn't see them. At the same time I realize that although I grew up without those things, I did grow up with a rich inheritance of people and places.

*Detroit. I'm thinking of you too, Philip Levine, you're not a poet of the academy either. You teach at universities, you teach literature and poetry, but I'm talking about yourself. You're a working man. You went to school, but you also did work with your hands.*

I went to a city university, Wayne University in Detroit. At that time it was not a state university. Today I think it's a kind of second-rate imitation of the University of Michigan. When I went there it was run by Wayne County, and it really functioned as a school for the city. They had an enormous night program that allowed people who worked all day long to take a full program in the afternoon and evening. I was able to go to college because the school welcomed working-class people, and I think that's not quite true anymore.

*Did you go nights?*

Some semesters I went nights.

*What kind of work did you do?*

I started working at about fourteen. It was during World War II. All you had to do was lie about your age, and you could get a job. They were dying to find people to work, and I worked at an incredible variety of dumb jobs. I worked in an ice factory, I worked in a bottling corporation, I worked on the railroad, I worked for Railway Express, I worked for Cadillac, for Chevrolet Gear and Axle, Wyandotte Chemical, just a tremendous variety of dumb jobs.

*So all this is reflected in your poetry, one way or another.*

Yes, several things happened to me, I think, as a guy doing those jobs. One was a determination not to spend my life this way, a terrific generating power that drove me back again and again to college because I just couldn't see living this way.

*But poetry. It wasn't the short story or the novel or the essay, it was the poem.*

Well, it was also those too. The first things I ever wrote were poems. I didn't know they were poems because like most American kids going to public schools my introduction to poetry was terrible. I mean I was introduced to poems that were totally irrelevant to my life. You know, "Snowbound." I had no real interest, and then we went "baDA baDA baDA" with the poems and learned the meters. For several years I tried the novel. I wrote two novels, which fortunately don't exist anymore. I think they were probably terrible. My temperament wasn't suited to fiction, so finally I came back to poetry, my first love. It wasn't until I was twenty-four that I said, "I'm going to leave this city, I'm going to leave this job, and I'm going to try to make it as a poet."

*The title poem of* They Feed They Lion *deals with a certain event in Detroit, a certain race riot.*

This poem is a response to the insurrection of 1967. I also have a poem that deals with what was simply a race riot that took place during my boyhood.

*That was during World War II, if I recall.*

Yes, that's correct. It grew up largely over the struggle for housing. There were maybe a million landless people who came from the South to work in the factories.

*Henry Ford brought up a lot.*

Yes, it started in the thirties, but it really got going wildly during World War II, and because of the freeze on buildings there was no place for these people to live, so public housing was constructed. Every time a housing tract was completed there came this thorny decision: will it be white or will it be black? I don't ever remember any serious discussion that it would be both. As you might suspect, the first several were white. Finally one was offered to black people, and that I think is what precipitated the riots. Wayne University has done a good study of the riot and the contribution the police made to it. Rather than impeding it, they speeded it up. The poem is really a poem centered around three things. One is my son, my youngest son coming of age, coming to look like a man. He's still quite young in the poem, but he's very strong and powerfully built, and I see him entering the world of men, the world of violence, and that frightens me. And I relive my own adolescence, which includes that race riot. His coming to fifteen reminds me of my coming to fifteen, and I have a lot of fear for him. Would you like me to read the poem? It's called "New Season," and it's also about my mother turning seventy. By the way, it takes place in California, and "hardpan" is a term we use out there to signify a certain kind of clay you have to dig through or dynamite through to plant trees. [Philip Levine reads the poem "New Season."]

*New Season*

My son and I go walking in the garden.
It is April 12, Friday, 1974.
Teddy points to the slender trunk
of the plum and recalls the digging
last fall through three feet
of hardpan and opens his palms
in the brute light of noon, the heels
glazed with callus, the long fingers
thicker than mine and studded with
silver rings. My mother is 70 today.
He flicks two snails off a leaf
and smashes them underfoot
on the red brick path. Saturday,
my wife stood here, her cheek cut
by a scar of dirt, dirt on her bare
shoulders, on the brown belly,
damp and sour in the creases
of her elbows. She held up a parsnip
squat, misshapen, a tooth pulled
from the earth, and laughed
her great white laugh. Teddy talks
of the wars of the young, Larry V.
and Ricky's brother in the movies,
on Belmont, at McDonald's,
ready to fight for nothing, hard,
redded or on air, "low riders,
grease, what'd you say about my mama!"
Home late, one in the back seat,
his fingers broken, eyes welling
with pain, the eyes and jawbones
swollen and rough. 70 today, the woman

66

who took my hand and walked me
past the corridor of willows
to the dark pond where the one swan
drifted. I start to tell him
and stop, the story of my 15th spring.
That a sailor had thrown a black baby
off the Belle Isle Bridge was
the first lie we heard, and the city
was at war for real. We would waken
the next morning to find Sherman tanks
at the curb and soldiers camped
on the lawns. Damato said he was
"goin downtown bury a hatchet
in a nigger's head." Women
took coffee and milk to the soldiers
and it was one long block party
till the trucks and tanks loaded up
and stumbled off. No one saw
Damato for a week, and when I did
he was slow, head down, his right arm
blooming in a great white bandage.
He said nothing. On mornings I rise
early, I watch my son in the bathroom,
shirtless, thick-armed and hard,
working with brush and comb
at his full blond head that suddenly
curled like mine and won't
come straight. 7 years passed
before Della Daubien told me
how three white girls from the shop
sat on her on the Woodward Streetcar
so the gangs couldn't find her
and pull her off like they did
the black janitor and beat
an eye blind. She would never
forget, she said, and her old face
glows before me in shame
and terror. Tonight, after dinner,
after the long, halting call
to my mother, I'll come out here
to the yard rinsed in moonlight

that blurs it all. She will not
become the small openings
in my brain again through which the wind
rages, though she was the ocean
that ebbed in my blood, the storm clouds
that battered my lungs, though I hide
in the crotch of the orange tree
and weep where the future grows
like a scar, she will not come again
in the brilliant day. My cat Nellie,
15 now, follows me, safe
in the dark from mockingbird
and jay, her fur frost tipped
in the pure air, and together we hear
the wounding of the rose, the willow
on fire—to the dark pond
where the one swan drifted, the woman
is 70 now—the willow is burning,
the rhododendrons shrivel
like paper under water, all
the small secret mouths are feeding
on the green heart of the plum.

*I'm thinking as you read "New Season" the different dimensions to it. The event, the horrendous event, the frightening, the terrible and terror-evoking aspects of it. At the same time you think of the growth of your son and you worry about the world he's going to live in and the agedness, the aging of your mother.*

My hope in writing the poem—it was a wonderful experience writing the poem because I had in my mind these three powerful themes and my hope was that I could weave them together. When I wrote it all during one morning it felt right. And I said, "I did it!" and I'm not sure; time will tell me if I did it right. But that day I said, "I got it!"—it was a terrific experience, feeling that I had woven them together.

*I think there are so many poems that because of your own experience, the fact that you were working, a lot of these poems have the details—that's what I think about again, the details. I remember I was talking to a guy when I was working on this book* Working, *he was an auto worker in the deep South, a white guy. He had a Bible, lived in a trailer. But as he describes his day, it's in such detail, it's so dramatic. "What happens?" I say. "Well, I get up at 6:00, sometimes 6:15, and the radio clock's going. I open one eye, and I shut it to myself. I get up, and then I go to the bathroom and comb my one hair. Then I have a cup of coffee, it might be half a cup. You know, it's routine. I have a piece of toast; it might be two pieces, maybe half a piece. I kiss my wife; it's routine. I get in the car; it's routine. And I gotta go to the factory." Now if he comes a minute late he's docked half an hour. But as he describes this it's so dramatic! And he describes the details of getting there because the railroad crossings ... now if he misses one he's gonna be late because you wait fifteen minutes for those 100 cars to go by. So it becomes very dramatic! He's just describing each day. Now take an academician, some guy; I don't want to put down college people, I don't mean that at all. But it's abstract. He'll say, "Well, I get up; then I go to work." But to this guy who works with his hands—every detail! So, in a sense I'm thinking about your poetry and the fact that you've worked in all these plants and factories, which I'm sure plays a role in what Grace Shulman calls your eye and ear for the commonplace detail. It's so dramatic.*

Yes, it's very strange. It was at an early age, while I was working in factories and also trying to write. I said to myself, "Nobody is writing the poetry of this world here; it doesn't exist!" And it didn't. You couldn't find it. And I sort of took a vow to myself, which sounds kind of foolish in a way, but I'm not above foolishness. I took a vow that I was going to do it, and goddamn it, it didn't matter how long it was going to take. I was going to write the poetry of these people because they weren't going to do it. And it was very funny, when my fellow workers would say, you know, "What do you do?" and I would say, "I write poetry," nobody laughed at me. Nobody found it silly. Maybe they didn't understand what I was saying—I don't know—but nobody misused me for it. Nobody said *Doctor* or *square head* . . .

*Or* sissy . . .

No.

*By the way, I'm just curious; do you ever read any of what you wrote to the guys that worked with you? Ever?*

I have shown several of these poems to guys I've worked with and given some of the books to men I've worked with. I don't honestly know their response. I mean they've thanked me, but they seemed a little shy. I think it's clear that we recognize that we're not the same people we were then. That the life I've gone on to live . . .

*You know I've asked that question because I think I find Philip Levine's poetry terribly moving and beautiful and lyrical and at the same time, it's* There's the pavement. *I think because there's a young Englishman, a working man, in a beautiful book called* Aikenfield *by Ronald Blythe . . .*

Oh, a beautiful book!

*. . . in which he covers the villages. And this guy, David Collier his name is, and I paraphrase him badly. He says, You know, I think a young town boy (he was a working boy) can come into a place by accident, maybe an art gallery, just to get out of the rain, and as he watches that stuff he becomes a different person. And I always thought that the music of Mozart, serious classical music, was too good for me. I wasn't worthy of it. And then as I began to hear and I began to enjoy it, I said, "I am worthy of this," you know.*

Yes.

*And so I think to me this is the most telling comment I've heard in a long time, from this guy in Aikenfield. That's why I asked about these guys you worked with. My feeling is—and perhaps I'm a romantic—but I think it would be dug, what you write. What you write. In a sense you are commemorating their lives and your own, of course.*

For example, when I go to public schools, universities, or even high schools, and I meet young people from these backgrounds, I get to them. I reach them, and I'm more comfortable with them than say if I go to read at Princeton or Brown or those schools where I think I'm seen as a bit odd. You know, I mean, "wasn't poetry meant for us, not him." That kind of thing. Isn't poetry aloof and beautiful? Where's the beauty in this? And they don't see the beauty, say, in the perfection of capturing an experience. That's where the beauty lies. But some of the surfaces of these poems are kind of ugly. I mean, they deal with what is ugly, with punishing lives. I think the hardest thing for me to come to understand, and for young people I know whose backgrounds are similar, is that our lives, any life, is worthy of poetry. The experience of any human being is worth poetry.

*As you talk, you're setting this off in me. . . . During the Montgomery marches I met Molly Dobbs. Molly Dobbs is a very eloquent woman who had little schooling, and finally she went to college, the only one of her whole southern white family. And she hates the word "redneck." And she says, "These are poor, white people." And again the stereotype. And her people lived in the hill country, not the bottom land, the hill country. They were very poor, but they were taught to respect others. And she says, "The greatest mistake George Wallace has ever made is to allow poetry in the schools." Of course she was a kid. Her whole life changed when she read Gray's "Elegy." Gray's "Elegy" changed her entire life. And she sees the poetry, and she says that certain poems such as (I'll say) Philip Levine's are absolutely understood by people and move them terribly. And she said George Wallace's greatest mistake is allowing poetry in the schools.*

That's marvelous.

*You say you're a political person, a political poet. How would you describe a political poet?*

Well, I think a political poet is one who doesn't necessarily tell people how to vote or how to think and what specific attitudes they should have, but he or she's a poet who deals with the political facts of our lives, that for example we live at the pleasure of people with enormous power and very little compassion. And that there is very little justice in the world, and that most of what young people are told, and older for that matter, about the nature of this country, this America, is nonsense. We are told that the constitution is some kind of holy document; it was written by people who owned slaves. We're told that there is something holy about the state. Originally, I think people banded together for protection, but now we see that the state is our largest enemy. It has, on several occasions, brought us close to destruction, and it may still. And I feel, as a poet, that one of my functions is constantly to remind people of this. I think, too, that just the writing of a poem is a political act. I don't think there is anything more clear than the fact that our politicians are murdering our language. I mean they misuse our language constantly, and they all lie anyway. They talk about their "credibility gaps," which is just a euphemism for a lie. I think that if a man or a woman insists on depicting the truth, that in itself is a kind of political act. If, for example, I write a poem about a tree, and I try to tell you it's unique and lovable, I'm going to interfere with the fact that you're going to cut it down and reduce it to so many board feet, so I've already entered the arena of politics.

*So if you write about a beautiful lake. . .*

Yes. . .

*. . . by the very nature of its being polluted. . .*

. . . yes. . .

*. . . by industrial waste or military waste. . .*

That's right. . .

*. . . it's political.*

That's right.

*You'd be saying the very air we breathe is political though polluted.*

Look, we're told that we're the richest people in the world. We have this country that's so rich. You live in California and try to walk on it. You get your ass shot off. I mean there are signs all over saying No Trespassing. I mean is it ours really? I mean how much of it is ours? They took the air away. They took the water away. They took the mountains away. They took it all away. And they sold it. And so I think the word "political" is enormous, and I don't think any poet, if he's true to what he sees and loves, can pursue his poetry without being to a degree political in today's world. Because there isn't anything the powers that be don't want to take and sell. And no matter what you love, you don't want to see it misused. They intend its misuse.

*And of course you think of Chile, naturally.*

Yes, you think of Chile, and one knows America's involvement in it and how we cooperated in bringing down the. . .

*And of course they had a poet who was highly political.*

Yes, Victor. . .

*No, I was thinking of Pablo Neruda.*

Oh, yes, they had the giant, maybe the greatest American poet. It's ironic that maybe the two greatest American poets of the twentieth century were not from the United States. But they were Pablo Neruda and Cesar Vallejo of Peru, both intensely political poets.

*But just a moment ago you were saying Victor Jara.*

Yes, Victor Jara was a young man who sang his poems.

*He was a sort of Woody Guthrie, in a way, of Chile.*

Yes, except unlike Guthrie he had an enormous following during his life.

*During his own life?*

Yes, he inspired a great many people during his own life, and he became a dangerous man, in his way.

*At which point the military junta killed Victor Jara. He was arrested by the junta after the murder of Allende, and he was in the football field that became a big prison camp. They knew he was dangerous because of his songs and poetry.*

Yes.

*Which is again political. Would you read your poem. . . .*

"For the Poets of Chile." I say "poets" because Neruda died right after the insurrection. [Philip Levine reads "For the Poets of Chile."]

### For the Poets of Chile

Today I called for you,
my death, like a cup
of creamy milk I
could drink in the cold dawn,
I called you to come
down soon. I woke up
thinking of the thousands
in the *futbol* stadium
of Santiago de Chile,
and I went cold, shaking
my head as though
I could shake it away.
I thought of the men
and women who sang
the songs of their people
for the last time, I
thought of the precise
architecture of a man's wrist
ground down to powder.
That night when I fell asleep
in my study, the false
deaths and the real blurred
in my dreams. I called
out to die, and calling
woke myself to the empty
beer can, the cup
of ashes, my children
gone in their cars,
the radio still moaning.
A year passes, two,
and still someone must
stand at the window
as the night takes hold
remembering how once
there were the voices
of play rising
from the street,
and a man or woman
came home from work

humming a little tune
the way a child does
as he muses over
his lessons. Someone
must remember it over
and over, must bring
it all home and rinse
each crushed cell
in the waters of our lives
the way a god would.
Victor, who died
on the third day—
his song of outrage
unfinished—and was strung
up as an example to all,
Victor left a child,
a little girl
who must waken each day
before her mother
beside her, and dress
herself in the clothes
laid out the night
before. The house sleeps
except for her, the floors
and cupboards cry out
like dreamers. She goes
to the table and sets out
two forks, two spoons, two knives,
white linen napkins gone
gray at the edges,
the bare plates,
and the tall glasses
for the milk they must
drink each morning.

Shortly after this book came out I got a letter from England, it was a short letter, and it thanked me for writing "For the Poets of Chile," and for memorializing Victor in the poem. I couldn't read the signature, it was a very mannered signature. I stared at it and stared at it, and finally I figured it out—it was Joan Jara—it was Victor's widow. I was enormously moved by that. You know another curious thing that war did, it touched another one of my poems. I have another poem in the same book called "Elegy for Teddy Holmes, Dead in a Far Land," and it appeared originally in the *New Yorker* magazine. A woman wrote me a letter from New York, and she said her son had been killed in Chile and that she and her husband were inconsolable for a year. Then she came across this poem in which I spoke of the death of a very close friend a long way off. And she realized that other people survive these losses—although I think her loss was far greater than mine—and she thanked me for writing the poem.

*Where was Teddy Holmes killed?*

Teddy Holmes died in Ireland. But what really affected me the most was how meaningful poetry is to ordinary people. That it helps ordinary people get through their lives. It adds a dimension to their lives. For the most part we think of it as irrelevant because much of our poetry in English was written by courtiers to be read by kings and queens.

*You know, there's a Brecht poem that I paraphrase very badly. It's about the anonymous who are never written about, there's no poetry about them. It goes something like, Who built the seven gates of Thebes, where did the masons go who built the Chinese wall? Where did they go for lunch? (And this part I like.) When the Spanish Armada sank we read that King Philip wept. Were there no other tears? So this is what you're saying.*

There were a lot of widows and orphans.

*They are the noncelebrated, and in a sense you are celebrating the anonymous.*

That's right. That's my dearest hope—that I give them names. When I say, *The Names of the Lost*, when I titled my book that, I'm trying to give them their names back. . . .

*It's not simply that your poems go back to your memories, whether it's your grandmother or your grandfather or the guy you saw on the streetcar or working—they're all related.*

Yes. Like let me read this crazy little poem which came out of an actual experience of walking down the street. As a young kid in Detroit growing up I was nuts about jazz. You said you didn't feel worthy of Bach and Mozart; at first I didn't seem worthy of jazz, it was too complicated and marvelous, but I listened long enough and got to love it. And one day, I'd seen Art Tatum the night before playing in a concert. His plane had been late, and we waited for hours for him to come. It was worth it because when he got there he played for a long time and he played with extraordinary beauty. The next night I was walking down the street, and I saw him. For a moment I hesitated whether or not to go up and thank him for what he'd done. When I went over close to him I heard him talking about baseball, and I was so fascinated by what he was talking about I just walked behind him and said nothing and listened to this conversation about baseball, which was the last thing . . . I thought he'd be talking about music or some high and mighty thing. Let me read the poem; it's called "On the Corner." [Philip Levine reads "On the Corner."]

### On the Corner

Standing on the corner
until Tatum passed
blind as the sea,
heavy, tottering
on the arm of the young
bass player, and they
both talking
Jackie Robinson.
It was cold, late,
and the Flame Show Bar
was crashing
for the night, even
Johnny Ray
calling it quits.
Tatum said, Can't
believe how fast
he is to first. Wait'll
you see Mays
the bass player said.
Women in white furs
spilled out of the bars
and trickled toward
the parking lot. Now
it could rain, coming
straight down. The man
in the brown hat
never turned his head up.
The gutters swirled
their heavy waters,
the streets reflected
the sky, which was
nothing. Tatum
stamped on toward
the Bland Hotel, a wet

newspaper stuck
to his shoe, his mouth
open, his vest
drawn and darkening.
I can't hardly wait, he said.

*And so there is Tatum. It's funny you mention that. I remember running into Tatum—but you made a poem out of it—and though he was blind he loved hearing the radio baseball games. The time I ran into him it was spring training, and he listened to all the spring training games being broadcast. By the way, if we could just touch on this a moment. It's something you caught. Accident plays a role, doesn't it? It's something you happened to hear him say. So we talk about accident in art, don't we? Or circumstance.*

Oh, yes. Our lives, it seems to me, are just a series . . . I mean that's how I regard my life. I have a recent poem in which I say, If someone were going to tell me the meaning of my life, I'd turn away and not listen. I'd rather live it the way I'm living it, without understanding it. My poetry has taken me to a lot of places, a lot of odd places. Back in the late sixties—my kids were coming of draft age—and my wife, who is an American Indian, is an extraordinarily moral person, and she just wasn't going to give her kids to the army. So she and I and the kids went to live in Spain. People in California would write,"How can you live in Spain if you're so anti this kind of regime?" And I'd write back and say, "Well, you can hardly tell the difference between California and Spain, with California under Reagan." But the truth of the matter was it was the only place we could afford to live because it was cheap as hell. And one of the other reasons—I went there for two other reasons—one was to learn the language which had given us this great poetry in the twentieth century. And the third reason was that out of my childhood there were strong linkups to Spain. I was a boy during the Spanish Civil War. It was the most meaningful war I can remember. Many people from my neighborhood, in Detroit, went off to fight for a free Spain, and most of them who went didn't come home. I'd like to read a poem now about one of those men, who was the older brother of my closest friend at the time. It's called "To P. L., 1916–1937, a soldier of the Republic."

### To P. L., 1916–1937

a soldier of the Republic

Gray earth peeping through snow,
you lay for three days
with one side of your face
frozen to the ground. They tied your cheek
with the red and black scarf
of the Anarchists, and bundled you
in canvas, and threw you away.
Before that an old country woman
of the Aragon, spitting on her thumb,
rubbing it against her forefinger,
stole your black Wellingtons,
the gray hunting socks, and the long
slender knife you wore
in a little leather scabbard
riding your right hip. She honed it,
ran her finger down the blade, and laughed,
though she had no meat to cut,
blessing your tight fists
that had fallen side by side
like frozen faces on your hard belly
that was becoming earth. (Years later
she saw the two faces

at table, and turned from the bread
and the steaming oily soup, turned
to the darkness of the open door,
and opened her eyes to darkness
that they might be filled with anything
but those two faces squeezed
in the blue of snow and snow and snow.)
She blessed your feet, still pink,
with hard yellow shields of skin
at heel and toe, and she laughed
scampering across the road, into
the goat field, and up the long hill,
the boots bundled in her skirts,
and the gray hunting socks, and the knife.
For seven weeks she wore the boots
stuffed with rags at toe and heel.
She thought she understood
why you lay down to rest
even in snow, and gave them to a nephew,
and the gray socks too.
The knife is still used, the black handle
almost white, the blade
worn thin since there is meat to cut.
Without laughter she is gone
ten years now,
and on the road to Huesca in spring
there is no one to look for you
among the wild jonquils, the curling
grasses at the road side,
and the blood red poppies, no one
to look on the farthest tip
of wind breathing down from the mountains
and shaking the stunted pines you hid among.

*I was thinking about this poem. This is what Grace Shulman of the* Nation *talks about of Philip Levine's poetry. The details of this very poem, the poem you read just now, the elegy, a beautiful eulogy to a soldier of the Republican Army. She writes of my guest's poetry, ". . . it is the place he lived and died in that the poet describes in a lyrical ironic manner . . ." and then the details:*

> and on the road to Huesca in spring
> there is no one to look for you
> among the wild jonquils, the curling
> grasses at the road side,
> and the blood red poppies, no one
> to look on the farthest tip
> of wind . . .

*Just the idea of the place. She talks about what Mazzocco talks about in his tribute to you in the* New York Review of Books. *Again this matter of place, of person and the place.*

Yeah.

*This goes back to the beginning. You were saying, the landmarks, the places are going.*

That's right. They're going, and they mean everything to me. Let me read one final poem which is my most recent poem, just for the heck of it. It's a love poem, and love is a subject to which I'm turning now, and one that I have written very little about earlier. The *you* in the poem is my wife, and it's called "Toward Home."

*Toward Home*

> The years are turning
> toward home, and I
> am entering the forest
> of no trees, the winds
> that bring neither heat
> or rain. No bigger

than the stone you kicked
out of your way, still
I am all there is
of someone who lived
beside the great sea
and listened to its prayers.
Do you remember how
once you took my hand
and led me to a white room
I'd never seen before?
You held me close and said
my name again and again,
although the name was
wrong, the name of someone
I never was. Do you
recall that night? I was
awake even before the light
had moved from between
the leafless trees
and entered the dusty window
and touched your face open
beside me. How long ago
was it? I slipped out
from between the clean sheets
and stood naked and cold
on the bare wood floor
sorting my clothes from yours,
needing to return to a life
that was no more me
than any other life,
to a room I paid for
and so could say was mine,
to a blue work shirt softened
with use and bearing a name
that also was not mine.
In the mirror I saw
a body, mine, thickened
with years of work but still
soft and shadowed in those
small valleys where so few
hands had strayed, a body

you said had grown precious
in its deformities. Even
then, combing my tangled hair
with the hardened fingers
with which I stained
the world, I inhaled
the perfume of our sweat
and thought, No one
will ever shape my face
so perfectly or hold
so much of me in her eyes
and name it all. And no one
ever has. All those years
ago, I walked in the frozen
January air, chanting
my happiness to no one
along the curving road
that led toward town,
that led toward manhood,
toward you again and again,
toward age, madness, this
coming to be the salt
the sea would crust
over the eyelids of
my closed face, toward
the pebble washed ashore,
the moon that turned
its face away, toward
everything for which there
were no names, no open hands,
no voice to even try.

*Thanks for that poem. By the way, when you said it's a theme you haven't touched on before, the theme of love, I could disagree with you. You have in a tangential way.*

Oh, sure. I meant romantic love between men and women, sexual love.

*Are you turning inward? I hate to use that phrase.*

Yes, to a degree. But I think that the speaker in my poems isn't me. He's anybody. When I'm most pleased with a poem, it's not me talking, it's anybody.

*Of course, this is precisely the mark of the poet, isn't it? That it's beyond himself. Of course the fact that these guys or it could be the kid in college or the old dowager or the old charwoman . . .*

Yeah. If it isn't for all of them . . .

*Yeah . . .*

. . . to hell with it.

*Philip Levine is my guest, and you've heard just a few of his poems and his reflections. It's been a delight having you. This has been a rocking chair show for me in which I know my guest is articulate and eloquent, and I've got little to do, and I love it. Any thought before we say goodbye for now?*

Well, let me tell you something. When I was living in Spain, the book that meant the most to me, believe it or not—you might as well believe it. The thing that I missed the most was the American language. It really drove me nuts not to hear my fellow Americans. And I used to read your book, *Division Street*, over and over, not for the point it was making but just to hear Americans talk. That was 1965, 1966. And when I left I gave the book to another American writer who just wanted it so bad. Just had to hear those voices.

*Well, that's very good to hear.*

It's part of the wealth.

*But they are the voices. That's precisely the point. I suppose that's one of the reasons I go so much for your writing. Thank you very much, Philip Levine.*

Thank you, Studs.

# Interview with Calvin Bedient

Los Angeles, California, Winter, 1977

*On the Murder of Lieutenant José del Castillo by the Falangist*
*Bravo Martinez, July 12, 1936*

When the Lieutenant of the Guardia de Asalto
heard the automatic go off, he turned
and took the second shot just above
the sternum, the third tore away
the right shoulder of his uniform,
the fourth perforated his cheek. As he
slid out of his comrade's hold
toward the gray cement of the Ramblas
he lost count and knew only
that he would not die and that the blue sky
smudged with clouds was not heaven
for heaven was nowhere and in his eyes
slowly filling with their own light.
The pigeons that spotted the cold floor
of Barcelona rose as he sank below
the waves of silence crashing
on the far shores of his legs, growing
faint and watery. His hands opened
a last time to receive the benedictions
of automobile exhaust and rain
and the rain of soot. His mouth,
that would never again say, "I am afraid,"

closed on nothing. The old grandfather
hawking daisies at his stand pressed
a handkerchief against his lips
and turned his eyes away before they held
the eyes of a gunman. The shepherd dogs
on sale howled in their cages
and turned in circles. There is more
to be said, but by someone who has suffered
and died for his sister the earth
and his brothers the beasts and the trees.
The Lieutenant can hear it, the prayer
that comes on the voices of water, today
or yesterday, from Chicago or Valladolid,
and hangs like smoke above this street
he won't walk as a man ever again.

*Of the various politics of the left, you prefer anarchism?*

Yeah. I hate communism.

*Why is that?*

Well, as we see it say in the Soviet Union it seems to
me it isn't based on brotherhood anymore. It's a loy-
alty to a code or really to a bureaucracy and if some-
one's declared disloyal to the bureaucracy, even if
he's your brother, you're given a little slip and told
to kill him and you do it. It doesn't seem to me that
it has much to do with—with, say, communal ideals,
or egalitarian communalism, or whatever you want
to call it. It seems to me to betray completely the
idealism of the people who were involved in it in the
nineteenth century. It seems as ugly as what we offer
the world.

*Do you think anarchism has much relevance to Americans
today?*

Yeah. I'm not so naive that I think it's going to come to power—even that phrase is kind of a silly one when you think of it, because it's the annihilation of power. It's an enormously useful belief, judging from what it's done for me and the way I feel about myself, the way I feel about the people I know, and how I've seen it affect my wife, who caught the disease from me, and some of my friends. I think it's an extraordinarily generous, bountiful way to look at the universe. It has to do with the end of ownership, the end of competitiveness, the end of a great deal of things that are ugly.

*It's a truer communism than Communism, then.*

That's right. Because as an anarchist one's loyalty is to people, finally.

*Is there an incongruity between loyalty to people and the size of America, do you think?*

Oh, yeah. I agree. I don't see how it's going to take place. I don't believe that America will ever be an anarchist nation. I'm not waiting for . . . I'm not a Spanish anarchist, I'm not going to declare the kingdom of heaven on earth.

*But anarchism can open up sympathies, at least.*

I think so. It's the only politics that have any attraction for me.

*When you were a kid you talked about Ferrer Guardia?*

Yes. He was a hero. There's something that the history books often refer to as the Terrible Week, because the history books are written by capitalists. And he had a free school in Spain, and he was considered a terrible troublemaker because of this. And a guy who worked for his school went to Madrid and tried to assassinate the . . . king's son who had just gotten married. . . . The school was closed, and he left—but he wasn't tried or anything—he left Spain. And he returned . . . about two weeks before an uprising in Barcelona which lasted a week. . . . Ferrer was picked up along with a number of other people, but he was never in Barcelona during this uprising. And I think he was tried on Friday, sentenced on Saturday, executed on Monday. . . .He had no chance. He became a hero to a lot of working-class people. . . .

*To your father, for example?*

No, my father was apolitical. But to older men in my neighborhood that I knew very well, especially two Italians who ran a cleaning and dyeing operation down on my corner who were anarchists, and whom I used to talk to all the time. I was fascinated by their politics. And they had a communist working for them, and they had these violent arguments. He was a real communist; he had two sons, one was called Lenin, one was called Stalin. I was about thirteen and listening to these guys screaming at one another.

*So would you say that your obsession with the Spanish Civil War began with these anarchists down the street?*

Even earlier. It began because it was apparent to me . . . coming from a Jewish household, I had a very heightened sense of what fascism meant. It meant anti-Semitism; it meant Hitler. I mean he was like the king fascist. And then there were these minor league fascists, but they essentially meant the same thing. And I saw the threat reaching right into my house and snuffing me out if something wasn't done to stop the advance of fascism. And Detroit was an extraordinarily anti-Semitic city. I don't know if you're aware of a man named Father Coughlin, who was on the radio every Sunday from Royal Oak, which is a suburb of Detroit. He had a huge church out there and he preached Hitler every Sunday. I spent most of my childhood and adolescence fighting with people who, you know, wanted to beat me up because I was Jewish. I didn't enjoy it at all. Even winning wasn't very satisfying, you weren't winning anything. So my obsession with the Spanish Civil War began during the civil war itself, which began when I was very young. The things I was hearing everywhere were true, that the Nazis and the Italians were there supporting the fascist army, and it was just more of the advance of fascism, which had already claimed Austria and during the Spanish Civil War took Czechoslovakia and began to move in on Poland, demanding the Polish Corridor. So that you didn't know where this threat was going to end. And so-called western democracies were doing a pathetic job of combating it. They were looking the other way. And if you look into the history you know that they wanted fascism to succeed. It was a way of eliminating communism . . .

*You refused to serve during the Korean War, I understand. Were your reasons highly rationalized at the time—principled?*

Yeah, I think they were. I had no faith in what I was being told about the war. I remembered after all, during World War II, all the propaganda that we read, everything we were told about these extraordinarily noble Russian people, who were now our allies. And within two or three weeks after the end of the war I was reading in the newspapers notions about dropping the atomic bomb on Moscow and wiping out the Commies. I was so disillusioned by this. And I was Russian in my own origin. But I didn't believe anything I read in the newspapers or anything my government said. . . . I had no idea why we were in Korea. I had the feeling that it had something to do with why we fought every war we ever fought—for empire, for gain, except for the few where we were attacked, as in the War of 1812. But it seemed to me it was probably like all the other wars; it was just to advance the American market. And I didn't have an enemy in Korea, there wasn't anybody there I wanted to hurt. And I also had something I wanted to do: I wanted to write poetry. It seemed important to me; it seemed a lot more important than taking my life out and letting Uncle Sam shred it, you know. So I said no.

*Did the government punish you in some way?*

Only for a few days. I mean they put me under psychiatric observation, and after a few days announced to me that I was psychotic. And released me. But I ought in all fairness to say the people who said I was psychotic knew I wasn't; they were doing me a terrific favor. For which I'm eternally grateful. . . . I'm not too sure about that; I know they didn't want any trouble—I mean they didn't want the publicity; I think that was part of it. I didn't read about any kind of draft resistance during the Korean War, and yet there must have been a lot; but it never got in the newspapers. Probably because they just sent the guys home. I mean I had a little card that said 4 F, Psychotic. And I wasn't any more psychotic than . . . I was holding down a job.

*How did the subject of "On the Murder of Lieutenant José del Castillo by the Falangist Bravo Martinez, July 12, 1936" come to you?*

It came to me mistakenly. It's an interesting story. José del Castillo's death, I believed, was one in a series of deaths that led to the death of García Lorca. That's what I read in one of the older histories of the Spanish Civil War . . . he was killed because there was a large building strike in Madrid—construction workers were striking—and right-wing newspapers were urging action against these strikers, saying it was outrageous that they were slowing down this building, etc. And what in Spain is called a señorito, which means a rich young man—these señoritos were riding around in their cars and stopping at building sites and shooting these guys that were striking, and killing them. And del Castillo got involved in one of these incidents, and he killed a couple of señoritos. A note was thrown into his barracks saying that he was going to be killed. And on a particular Sunday, which was I think one week before the beginning of the Spanish Civil War, he was murdered right out in the open in a park in Madrid. I put him in Barcelona. I take the liberty that painters have always taken: to move the scene to a congenial one. I don't know Madrid. I never saw it as an energetic and lively and beautiful city. I saw it only under Franco. Just the way a Dutch painter puts the crucifixion in Holland, I said, "Hell, I'll move it, to a street of enormous energy and beauty, the Ramblas," which is my favorite street in the world. At any rate, to get back to the other thing, his fellow soldiers, policemen in the Guardia de Asalto wanted to revenge his death, so they went out and grabbed . . . a right-wing journalist of enormous importance, Calvo Sotelo. . . . And the story was, then, that that murder brought about the uprising, the civil war. And the story in the early history of the Spanish Civil War that I read was that García Lorca was then murdered . . . that his life was taken away, a writer for a writer. And I wrote the poem believing that.

Then along came Ian Gibson's book *The Death of Lorca* and it became perfectly clear that those guys would have killed him if he had turned into an angel. I mean they didn't give a shit about the journalist, Sotelo. They killed him . . . out of envy; they killed him the way people with no talent want to kill the person who's just extraordinary. . . . His bisexuality probably had something to do with it too. . . . Then when I saw what I had done, when I read the Gibson book, I was kind of glad. A great many poets have mourned the death of García Lorca, but nobody had ever mourned the death of José del Castillo in a poem; and so I'm sort of happy that I mourned him for the wrong reasons. They turned out to be the right reasons, in a way.

*One of your poems speaks of the laborers in Detroit as entering the fires, as if they were martyrs. Do you feel about laborers in the California fields the way you felt about the workers in the auto industry in Detroit? And what is it that you feel? Is it simply the sense that they're being insulted and injured?*

Yes, and it's also the sense (because I participated in it) of the extraordinary physical agony of that kind of brutal work. I mean, just so I could see what it was like I went out and spent a day . . . two days as an agricultural worker in California. The days were separated by years. But I wanted to see what one of those long, endless days was like. And it seemed to me just as agonizing a kind of work as the heaviest work I'd done . . . I used the word *fire*, I suppose, because I worked in a forge room for a long time, and you were dealing with metals that had been heated white hot. In a way you almost *were* entering fire, you see.

*Do you have any thoughts on why there seems to be so little political commitment in American poetry—at least in the poetry that lasts?*

There's some. I think there's too little, sure . . . I see it, of course, in Whitman. And I see it very powerfully in a lot of novelists: in Dreiser, Sherwood Anderson, Dos Passos at his best in *USA;* I see it .in Anderson's and Dreiser's poetry, too—it's terrible poetry but it has political commitment. I see it in Patchen very much. I see it in some of Rexroth, some of his best poems. And then there was some during the Vietnam war. A lot of poets got political for a short time.

*Is there something defused, or diffuse, about the American political situation that discourages poets from taking a strong political stand in their poetry?*

I think that's part of it. I think also that when you think about who's formed American poetry as it is now, you go back to, say, the Fugitives, you go back to Eliot, to Pound. The only politics they have are very conservative. Most of the poets are coming out of the universities too, and God knows they don't fool around with politics; I mean when they teach books they talk about structure and irony and things like that. And so I don't think people are encouraged to . . . and then we don't have to endure the kind of hell that a Latin American writer has to endure. We don't have to cope with censorship. The government here is much more efficient about the way it takes our money and takes our lives and our land and our water and our air. The Latin Americans are clumsy by comparison. They throw the poets in prison, they torture them, they break their hands, they shoot them. Here, they can write whatever they want. And all five thousand readers can read it and memorize it and it won't do a goddamn thing. They're not the kind of people who are going to go out and buy guns and shoot anybody. . . . We are so efficient that a poet can forget what poetry can do, it seems to me. I forgot what it can do for a long time.

*Are you writing political poetry now?*

Yes. I have been for many years. I think there came a point where I came back to my original reasons for wanting to write. Probably around 1964. Although when I look at even my first book I see—I don't know if you know the poem "The Negatives" in my first book. It's about French deserters from the French Algerian army, and there's a guy in there, an American, who has come back to the United States from Algeria, and he feels "caught in a strange country for which no man would die." And I must have written that when I was thirty. So I was aware of why I started to write . . . but without readers it seems pointless to keep raging about politics. If you don't have readers you're not going to change anything. . . . I began writing poetry to do something with it, to effect some kind of moral change; but without readers I knew I couldn't do that. Meanwhile I was writing it and I enjoyed writing it, and I got better. And the most wonderful times in my life were when I was inspired writing poetry.

*Do you feel a strong kinship with certain other poets in your generation? Do you feel closer, perhaps, to some dead poets?*

Yes, I think I feel closer to some dead poets. There are a couple of poets in my generation . . . I like a lot of them personally and I know them, some I like a great deal. And I like the work of many even though it isn't anything like mine . . . I'm glad they don't write like me; it would be very boring if everybody wrote like me. . . . There are certain poets who write poems that I wish I had written, because they're so beautiful. And they are about things that I'm concerned with. A few of Gary Snyder's poems strike me that way; a couple of Ginsberg's poems, a lot of Galway Kinnell's poems, of Jim Wright's, a lot of Denise Levertov's poems. . . . Some of the younger poets that I read—Laura Jensen, Louise Glück, Larry Levis, Michael Harper, Charles Wright: they don't write poems that I want to write, but I'm awfully glad that they're writing, because they write so goddamn well. But the poets that I derive from, none of them are my contemporaries, it seems to me.

*Would you name some names?*

In an article I wrote for an anthology I was in, I talked about the influence of Bly and Rexroth, and I've always regretted that. At the time I thought it was true, but as the years have gone on I think that it's not true and I should have kept my mouth shut and waited to see. . . . I think a poet who has had an enormous influence on me is Robert Penn Warren, because I'm a narrative poet almost always, and he was a narrative poet; and I love the way he put narrative into his poetry. . . . Patchen was another, in his better poems. . . . They too were narrative, like "The Orange Bears." And there are poets of other countries that I feel great kinship with: Zbigniew Herbert and Czeslaw Milosz, the Polish poets. Some of the Spanish poets. . . . But there are other poets I learned a great deal from, because they just wrote so goddamn well that I studied the way they did it. Hardy was a poet like that. I love Hardy; I think he's a great poet. I love the way he puts a poem together when he's hitting it. Yeats—I don't think I could sit in a room with Yeats for five minutes without hitting him, but my God the poems are just extraordinary. . . . And Stevens is such a snob. Williams and Whitman I feel great kinship with.

*Whitman I expected you to name.*

I forgot. He's my favorite poet.

*I hear an occasional line in your poetry that reminds me of Dylan Thomas.*

I'm afraid I do too.

*And there's a launched quality to some of your lines that is like Thomas's—like those in "A Refusal to Mourn" . . . But there's less vibrato, less blur. . . . One thing you may have in common with Merwin and Kinnell is a certain orphic drive—though "orphic" doesn't really tell one much. Paul Zweig, in a review of* They Feed They Lion *in* Parnassus *(Fall/Winter, 1972), said that American poets have begun to create a language of revelation. And he sees you as engaged in this—what Rilke called building God through the labor of seeing. . . . Is revelation a term that. . . .*

It doesn't distress me. I don't know if I'm trying to create a language. I've never really thought about that. In a curious way, I'm not much interested in language. In my ideal poem, no words are noticed. You look through them into a vision of . . . just see the people, the place. . . . Now obviously I'm never going to write my ideal poem, and maybe I'm talking about creating a language.

*You said in correspondence that you believe in romanticism—in all that bullshit. Are there aspects of romanticism that make you uneasy?*

I don't think that there are aspects of romanticism that make me uneasy. I grew up at a time when the word *romantic* was a dirty word, when the romantic poets were being thrown out of the window, so that we could all worship John Donne, John Crowe

Ransom, and poets of ahrny [irony], as Ransom used to say. But my favorite poet at that time was Keats, and I wasn't going to throw him out of the window for anybody.

I had the fortune or misfortune to spend one year of my life with Yvor Winters; and of course he wanted to heave all those guys out of the window in the worst goddamn way. For some dumb reason he picked me to come to Stanford on a writing grant; and when I got there he liked me personally, we got along pretty well; but he loathed my poetry. And that was a source of some satisfaction to me, because although I liked some of his poetry and I liked the way he had illuminated some Renaissance poetry, I wasn't really interested in the way he treated his contemporaries. And I wasn't interested in the poets he thought were gigantic in the twentieth century. I thought they were pretty puny, really. I remember once saying to him about Robert Frost, "You don't talk about a single one of his greatest poems. . . . You pick out his worst poems so that you can dismiss him. Is that fair?" And he said: "I wasn't trying to make him look good." Which was honest, but it told me where he was. He wasn't in the house of criticism that I felt was going to be useful to anybody. . . . He just scored a touchdown for neoclassicism or something. . . . So when I say "all that bullshit," I guess I'm sensitive to the fact that it has been written off as dreck. . . .

*Do you see yourself as being a poet who uses romanticism as a criticism of what we do to each other and what life does to us?*

Yeah. The Keats for example that I loved was the

Keats of the letters, not the poems, as much as I admire the odes. Because I think that he inherited a poetic tradition that was so puny that he could say, I would jump down Etna for any public good but I want to write beautiful poems. As though you couldn't perform a public good with poetry. And I think you can. . . . I mean, you think of all the misery that he saw and you read about it in his letters, and how little of it ever gets into his poetry. . . . He sits there for months while his brother Tom dies day by day of tuberculosis in what must have been one of the most polluted shitholes in the world, the London of the nineteenth century. And what does he get: "Here where men sit and hear each other groan, . . . Where youth grows pale, and spectre-thin, and dies." Tom gets two lines. And that's it. Bingo. I mean, I couldn't let America take my brother and kill him at seventeen or eighteen, and just sit there and say, "Well, I have to write poems about Grecian urns." Shit. I mean I don't think I'd ever get over it. And I don't think Keats wanted to get over it. I don't think that he inherited as strong a tradition as I did. He didn't *have* Whitman.

When I say I'm a romantic poet, it seems to me that I feel the human is boundless, and that seems to me the essential fact of romanticism.

*In "On the Murder of José del Castillo" you refer at the end to a kind of romantic hold-all that is beyond mortality altogether, transcendental. And this seemed to me rare in your work, where the romanticism is mostly immanent. Did you feel, "This is a departure for me, I'm walking out on a plank"?*

The poem originated in the ending. It just so happened that I was reading this book about José del Castillo and at the same time I was reading I had a very odd experience, which was a repetition of a youthful experience. I was driving on a Sunday morning and I turned on the radio and I heard a black preacher that I heard often when I was a kid. And this black preacher was talking in a way that was very familiar to me. And I got into the rhythm of what he was saying. . . . He was talking to people out there in the radio audience who couldn't be in the church because they were in one way or another hurt, sick, suffering. . . . And he was saying like, "Sally Benson, I know you're sick, I know you've had an operation. Hang on. We're praying for you." And then suddenly he said, "And you, Charles Something, old soldier, I know your wound. . . ." And then the problem became, How can I build a poem that will use this ending that I have in my head? . . . What I think I did was sit down and try to build a poem in which a man's death flows out from him. He dies, and his dying sort of goes out out out. And then what comes back is this prayer for him, back back back from the world. . . . That's what I saw as the structure that I had to create. I felt it was different from anything I'd ever done. I felt very excited about it. I mean, I went home and, man, I mean I was just, you know, flying, I knew I was going to get this son of a bitch.

*It's an exciting poem. It shares a quality that some of Robert Penn Warren's poems have: a kind of scattered sublimity, the scatteredness of sublimity. . . . Do you have any particular don'ts as a poet? What do you tell your students that they should try to avoid?*

One don't is never to defend your poetry against anybody. . . . A lot of what you hear is stupid, but you should keep your mouth shut and listen; you might learn something . . . And I tell my students that. Defend your right to be a poet . . . but not your poetry, because you'll stop people from trying to tell the truth. That's one. The other is never to follow the idea that got you to sit down and write the poem if the poem seems to be going someplace else. It knows better than you do. I don't see myself as the captain of the ship, if you can say that writing a poem is like taking a voyage or something . . . I don't think I'm the captain; I think I'm down in the hold throwing coal into the thing, trying to stoke it. . . . But I'm not a cabbage, I have a mind, and when I see suddenly that I'm writing something that William Carlos Williams writes, or something that I've already written, I say, "Hey, come on." My biggest danger is that I'll imitate myself. And that's the thing I—my wife is very good on that. She's very quick to point that out. And she's very precise in telling, in the way she does it . . .

*Your poetry contains few abstract statements. Is this because you agree with Edmund Burke that a clear idea is a little idea?*

I think part of it is that in a lot of poems (not my own) I'm aware of the fact that people create characters so that they can kill them and then make a point. And it seems to me that the people are more interesting than the point. And I don't want the characters in my poems giving up their lives so that a point can be made. . . . You know, abstract ideas are so monumental all the way from Plato to the present. They bore me. Philosophers bore me. I find them the most boring people I've ever come across in my life. I would much prefer spending, you know, an afternoon with a bunch of jockeys or car mechanics than with philosophers. I remember renting my house to a philosopher who let all the trees die. And when I got angry with him, because my wife planted those trees and loved them—seven trees he let die— he said, "I didn't think you were the kind of man who would care about something like that." And to me that was the voice of the philosopher—"something like that": a living thing.

*What question would you like an interviewer to ask you?*

Are you happy you became a poet?

*Are you happy you became a poet?*

Yes, very happy, and very surprised that I've gone as far as I've gone. . . . I had great ambitions but my hopes were small; and part of this was due to the fact that I came out of a situation where to say I'm a poet meant I'm nuts. . . . Yeah, I've liked my life in poetry for a number of other reasons, too. It's put me in touch with a lot of marvelous people that I've had a chance to meet because I was a poet. And I know a lot of terrific young people. I keep meeting new people because I travel around and give readings. . . . I would never have become a teacher without being a poet, because I wasn't interested in scholarship. And I enjoy teaching . . .

*I want to ask you about the extreme contrast between what*

*you call your buffoonery, the humor of your social personality, and the lyrical plangency of your poetry. Is the buffoonery a kind of defense for your vulnerability?*

I don't really like wise men, or wise women for that matter. I don't like those wisdom machines telling people how they ought to live. Some of them are poets, and they go around telling people how they ought to live. So I want to make it clear that I don't know how other people ought to live. . . . And I make this very clear through the humor . . .

*What Ashbery has done is put the seriousness and buffoonery together in the poems.*

Yeah. He said to me, "You probably think I'm frivolous." And I said, "No, John, I don't." And he insisted on it. And I insisted that I didn't feel that way. And then he said he liked my poetry a great deal but that I probably wouldn't believe it. And I said, "No, I believe it. I think it's pretty terrific myself. Why wouldn't I believe that you would like it?" And I said, "I like your poetry. I think you write with extraordinary brilliance." And Ashbery certainly is not a wisdom machine. I feel very sympathetic to him as a person. But there are a number of people who go around the country with a sort of program . . . they're gurus. And I'm not. I don't have the answer to anything, except, "Keep trying, kid, buddy, old man." Even though my poems are very serious, they're not answers.

# Interview with Jan Garrett

Sydney, Australia, Summer, 1978

*Are you teaching now?*

No, I'm here in Australia being extraordinarily lazy. I just finished teaching at Columbia University in New York City, and in the fall I'll be teaching at a branch of the State University of California.

*Oh, I see. You teach poetry? Or creative writing?*

Well, both, but mainly creative writing.

*What does that entail, teaching creative writing? That's always interested me.*

By and large it entails not trying to discourage people with talent from writing. And trying to get young people to be a little harder on themselves than they would ordinarily be. Trying to get them to look at their work with the idea that if it's going to last it has to be damn good. Young writers, middle-aged writers, and old writers all like just to fall back from their work with this sigh of fulfillment as if it were this big meal they'd just finished. And you have to prod, especially the young, toward the direction of saying, I can do better than this. One of the ways you do this is to give them things to read to try to widen their horizons. I mean, I'm always asked the question, "Can you teach people to write?" Obviously you can't teach people without talent to write. You can stop people from writing, and so the real trick is not to stop the talented. And also to stop some of the clods; it seems to me that's the hardest part of teaching. There are some people who should not devote their lives to literature. For all I know they might make great ballet dancers or guitarists or dishwashers. But they're not going to be writers no matter how long they try, and that's the hardest part, to say, "You know, honey, you just don't have it. Try something else."

*Unclog the parts so the very talented can get through.*

That's right.

*Do you find that the students you are teaching, the young students—I gather they are young, aren't they? They're not mature age students?*

By and large they're young. At Columbia I had people from twenty all the way to fifty, but that's an unusual situation. Usually they're in their early twenties.

*Do you find them less well read than the average writer was in your generation?*

Much less so, oh yeah.

*In what way?*

They watch television. They've been fooling around with TV and taking a lot of dope and listening to the Beatles and the Bee Gees. They've had at least one of their big eyes on pop culture. I mean I grew up in an age when there wasn't much to distract you from reading. I mean, if you wanted to enter a world that was more interesting than the world you lived in, the only way you could do it was with books. I mean the movies I saw as a kid were fairly hopeless. They were about the French Foreign Legion. Radio was good when it was funny. Comedians like Jack Benny and Fred Allen were very funny, but that was an hour a week between the two of them. If you really wanted to encounter people who were more interesting than your own people, you had to find them in books. And that's where I found them, but I don't find my young students nearly as well read as the kids I grew up with.

*Galway Kinnell said, when he was out here during writers' week, that young writers these days haven't been soaked in the King James version of the Bible. Which I suppose is probably true. And he thinks there's a great divide between those people like himself who were soaked in the King James version as well as other classics of English prose and poetry.*

Yes.

*A great divide between those and the younger generation of poets coming up who don't have those rhythms almost programmed into their literary heads. Do you find that too?*

Oh yes. There's no question about it. I mean when I

grew up I expected, for example, that I'd spend ten to fifteen years learning the craft of poetry. I had the years to spend too. I was in no hurry. It was the United States during the fifties which wasn't going any place except backward. And so to step out of society and to become a poet and somehow just survive seemed like a damn good idea at the time. I didn't want to take part in what America was doing, which was hounding down and persecuting people that they might accuse of being Communists. Or carrying on a war on the Asian mainland.

*In Korea?*

Yes. And I thought, my God, here I am in my early twenties and I'm very healthy. I'm going to outlive Keats by maybe fifty years, and I've got a hell of a lot of time to learn the craft of poetry. And in the city in which I grew up there were about two or three million people, and there were about eight of us writing poetry that I knew of. Today there would be two or three hundred writing.

*This was Detroit, Michigan?*

Yes. There would be two or three hundred writing poetry today. There would be magazines in Detroit publishing them. There were no magazines publishing us in Detroit twenty-five years ago. If you were going to be published you had to be published in Chicago or New York City or San Francisco, which were the centers of poetry then. Today poetry is scattered throughout the country. There's much wider interest, and so there's the possibility of early success, which didn't exist for someone from Detroit when I was young, and so there was nothing to tempt me toward immediate discovery, so I took my time.

*You felt you had ten years or more to read and learn what you've just called the craft of poetry. I presume that was when you were a factory worker and truck driver. Was it? When you were younger, according to the biographical details in Mark Strand's* Contemporary American Poets, *you were . . .*

I became a factory worker at the age of fourteen during World War II when anybody in Detroit could get a job because so many men had been drafted into the armed forces and there was such a demand for people to work in the war plants. And I kept working through college and after college. At the age of about twenty-six I was suddenly freed of a lot of financial burdens and I just decided, I'm going to work as little as possible and write as much as possible. I sort of switched my priorities and opted for poverty and poetry. I lived that way for a while, and then I began publishing widely and I went into academia because that was the easiest thing—I didn't want to work anymore, so I took a job teaching.

*Were you writing poetry before you were free of the obligation of working?*

Yes, but I wasn't able to devote nearly as much energy and time as later on. I was a slow learner, but I'm a very stubborn man, so once I got free of those burdens I could work six to eight hours a day.

*What started you writing poetry?*

Two things. One was that I lived in a very violent, tumultuous household. I would go out of the house in the evenings to escape everybody yelling at everybody else. I had no one to talk to, so I talked to no one, and in a way that's a form of poetry. I would have devoted these little oral compositions to the moon and stars if the moon and stars had ever been above Detroit, but the smog prevented me from speaking to them. I did that when I was thirteen and fourteen; I stopped about the time I got interested in girls. Instead of going out and talking to myself, I went out and talked to girls.

*In rhymed couplets?*

No, in the same incoherent prose. And with the same results: no one listened. And then during my last year of high school, a teacher, for some reason I never understood, handed me a book and suggested that I read it. It was the poetry of Wilfred Owen. This was during the latter stages of World War II, and I was faced with the draft; many of my fellow schoolmates had died already in the war, and I was terrified of the war. I was terrified of going to it, of being maimed by it, of killing other people. These were emotions that were unacceptable to me and to all of my friends. We never spoke about things like that; we never communicated on an honest level. No one said, "Aren't you scared?" But reading Owen I realized that all of my private feelings were shared and understood by someone else, and that these inadmissable, unacceptable feelings—the guys in the movies who had them were terrible people and always managed to get killed before the movie ended. Suddenly I saw that these were very human responses to a nightmarish situation, and I think it was then for the first time that the power of poetry meant a hell of a lot to me. That poetry was a kind of saving force, in my attitude toward myself: once my emotions became acceptable so was I to myself. It was shortly thereafter that I consciously sat down and tried to write poetry.

*You went to college. Was that after the war?*

Yes. I went to a city university, Wayne University in Detroit, which I think was a very good school—it was very good for me—because it reflected the character of the city. It wasn't trying to be the Harvard of Shitville, it was just trying to be what it was. It was open from eight in the morning until midnight so that men and women who worked any shift—we call them shifts, eight-hour shifts, three a day in the factories—any one of them could have gone to school full time. The city was there in the school; you were just as liable to be sitting next to a factory worker in his forties who might have been born in Hungary as you were to be sitting next to a nineteen-year-old beautiful girl wearing a short skirt. In that way it was a catastrophe. I always got seated next to the factory workers.

*So in that university, industry and academia had intercourse with one another probably in a literal and metaphorical sense.*

That's right. And in that way it made an education, say, in English literature not seem as hopelessly irrelevant as it actually was.

*Because of the interaction?*

Yes. Here we were sitting in the classroom pretending that it was important. That somehow life would change if we all read Milton, and we all read Milton, and nothing changed.

*You studied at one stage with Robert Lowell, didn't you?*

Yes, back in about 1952. I admired his poetry enormously, and so I just decided I'd go study with him. He was teaching at the University of Iowa, which was about 500 miles from where I lived. I went there, but I didn't have the money to enroll in school, so I just sat in on his classes for a semester. The next semester John Berryman was the teacher. He was an extraordinarily good teacher, the best teacher I'd ever had and the most inspiring force I ever came across to excite me about poetry. He made poetry seem enormously important at a time when nothing intellectual seemed very important in American life—right in the middle of the fifties. He was amazing . . .

*We reviewed, in fact Donald Davie reviewed, Berryman's collection of essays* The Freedom of the Poet. *You probably know the book.*

Yes, I know the book. Some of the essays were delivered as lectures to us, to the students back in 1953.

*Can you tell us a little bit about what Robert Lowell was like as a teacher?*

He was very boring. He was close to his second massive nervous breakdown, and I think he just didn't have the emotional or mental energy to give to us. As such, he was a lousy teacher. We all respected him enormously as a poet, and I think we were all very disappointed in how dull his classes were.

*What were his classes like?*

They were silence mostly. We'd ask a question and get nothing back; he's ask questions and not listen to the answers. It was that kind of thing. He was a man struggling to get through the hour. None of us knew this breakdown was ahead, so we were just sort of disgruntled and displeased with the classes. Within a month of the end of the semester he was in a mental institution, and then we understood why the classes had been so boring. I don't know what he was like as a teacher later in life; I've heard he was much better, but it wouldn't have taken much to be much better.

*Of course John Berryman has a reputation as having been a very good teacher. How did you find him?*

Extraordinary.

*What did he teach you?*

The first thing he taught me was that the writing of poetry no matter what the times were was an extraordinarily important thing. And if you gave your life to poetry, you gave it to something very important. He was familiar with an amazing range of poetry and a great range of languages, and he could bring to bear the excellence of poetry you'd never heard of. He was not, on the other hand, a pedant, standing above us. He shared his knowledge with us. He showed us, in a way, how to read a poetry that we'd turned our backs on and that we should have been attentive to.

*What sort of poetry was that?*

Whitman. Whitman's a good example. Whitman was kind of out in academia. Academia can't do a hell of a lot with Whitman: he's too clear. Academia requires a sort of Byzantine, closed world that it can invade and to some degree illuminate. Well, you can't do that with Whitman; he's right out front. I remember one of my teachers using the phrase about a person who liked Whitman; he called him a "Whitmaniac." So that while in public schools Whitman's dull poems were taught—"Song of the Open Road" and things like that—we never really looked at him in depth. Berryman would take a great poem like "Song of Myself" and spend a month on it. He'd read it in an extraordinarily powerful voice so you *had* to attend to it, and then he'd explicate the subtlest relationships of the sections to each other. He was totally excited by poetry; in class he'd start quivering and shaking with emotion. In a way, he was not built to last, and you know he didn't. But while he was here, he sure gave a lot.

*You said John Berryman taught you a lot about poetry and its importance. How did he think poetry was important?*

Well, in the sense that he was able to pick up the day's newspaper and say, here it is full of Eisenhower, John Foster Dulles, Joe McCarthy and the various American idiots of the time, and he'd say,

"Kids, this will pass. These idiots will be replaced by other idiots. Don't worry about it." And then he'd put alongside that paper the poems of John Keats and say, "This will not pass as long as our language is spoken. These poems will be read. Some things are transient and some things come close to being permanent. Don't lose sight of that." He was also able to read with extraordinary insight, not only famous or established poetry, but our poetry. He was very canny at separating our aims from our achievements and showing us where we fell short.

*So you were submitting your own poetry to him at the same time as . . .*

Oh, yes, he was teaching a writing workshop, and he was very brilliant in it. I think he was not overly generous with our work. I mean he was tough, and I think one of the things he taught me was to be tough with myself. Not to settle for what I first wrote, for what I first put on the page. He himself was very hard on his own work, and I think he passed that quality on to his own students. He was an ideal man for me to encounter at the time.

*So you felt he tightened up your work a lot. That he was tough with you. What else did he teach you?*

Well, he had a fantastic ear for poetry, and I think he'd written in about every form that English and American poets have used. And so he pushed and prodded us to develop our skills at the old meters, at accentual meters, at experimental meters and urged us too to gain greater control over the English sentence. These were all tools in the arsenal of poetry. When you were going to attack the bourgeois you'd better be equipped with a mastery of the English language. Because we had to get them before they got us, and all we had were words, so we'd better gain as much control over the use of language as we could. He was very eloquent in convincing us that this was necessary. Powerful feelings and a fountain pen weren't enough to make poems.

*What effect do you think it had over your own poetry, apart from tightening it and . . . ?*

One thing I needed to feel was that even if I failed to become a poet of some significance the attempt would be worth it. I may fail, I don't know, it's something that I don't spend hours thinking about, but I'm perfectly prepared to fail as a poet as long as it happens after I'm dead. I love being successful, but I don't confuse the kind of success I've had with excellence as a poet. I'm very successful right now, but that may just be a matter of being fashionable. Maybe the kind of poetry I write is in today and will be out tomorrow. I don't know. I know, for example, I'm in the *Oxford Book of American Poetry,* which just came out. They revise the book every twenty-five years. Now if I can die within twenty-four years I'll still be a monument. But I may be dropped in the next revision. Truthfully, I don't worry about that. I worry about writing the best I can. If it wasn't good enough, it wasn't good enough.

*Go as far as you can.*

Yes.

*You were working with and learning from Robert Lowell and John Berryman during the early fifties. In the early sixties you wrote some of the poems, at least two of the poems in the Mark Strand anthology I mentioned earlier, "On the Edge" and "The Horse."*

Yes. They're both from my first book, which is called *On the Edge.*

*Would you like to read one of the poems at this point?*

Let me read both of them because together they give a real sense of the two styles I was working in. "On the Edge" is an absolutely metrical poem; it's in rhymed iambic pentameter, and it's totally conventional in its verse structure. The other poem is experimental free verse, inspired by the work of William Carlos Williams. I think I could have written "On the Edge" without having read any twentieth century poetry. I could have been reading Wyatt—not Edgar Allen Poe—it's not that bad, Wyatt and maybe Pope. [Philip Levine reads "On the Edge."]

### On the Edge

My name is Edgar Poe and I was born
In 1928 in Michigan.
Nobody gave a damn. The gruel I ate
Kept me alive, nothing kept me warm,
But I grew up, almost to five foot ten,
And nothing in the world can change my weight.

I have been watching you these many years,
There in the office, pencil poised and ready,
Or on the highway when you went ahead.
I did not write; I watched you watch the stars

Believing that the wheel of fate was steady;
I saw you rise from love and go to bed;

I heard you lie, even to your daughter.
I did not write, for I am Edgar Poe,
Edgar the mad one, silly, drunk, unwise,
But Edgar waiting on the edge of laughter,
And there is nothing that he does not know
Whose page is blanker than the raining skies.

The other poem, "The Horse," is much more in the American tradition of free verse, especially that of Williams. [Philip Levine reads "The Horse."]

### The Horse

for Ichiro Kawamoto, humanitarian,
electrician, & survivor of Hiroshima

They spoke of the horse alive
without skin, naked, hairless,
without eyes and ears, searching
for the stableboy's caress.
Shoot it, someone said, but they
let it go on colliding with
tattered walls, butting his long
skull to pulp, finding no path
where iron fences corkscrewed in
the street and bicycles turned
like question marks.
     Some fled and
some sat down. The river burned
all that day and into the
night, the stones sighed a moment
and were still, and the shadow
of a man's hand entered
a leaf.
  The white horse never
returned, and later they found
the stableboy, his back crushed

by a hoof, his mouth opened
around a cry that no one heard.

They spoke of the horse again
and again; their mouths opened
like the gills of a fish caught
above water.
           Mountain flowers
burst from the red clay walls, and
they said a new life was here.
Raw grass sprouted from the cobbles
like hair from a deafened ear.

The horse would never return.

There had been no horse. I could
tell from the way they walked
testing the ground for some cold
that the rage had gone out of
their bones in one mad dance.

*Those two poems represent the the poles toward which you
write or the two different ways in which you write.*

In which I wrote.

*In which you wrote then.*

Yes. "The Horse" represents the direction I took. I
sort of gave up the other direction. My second book
is still made up of a lot of poems in traditional me-
ters and still very tightly controlled. But I think after
my second book I pretty much abandoned that style.

*Why did you abandon it?*

I got bored with what I'd already mastered, I think.
I mean, I felt I'd covered this ground with some

success, and I could do it. So now that I could do it, let me try doing something that I can't do. And I found that there were a lot of other things ahead in free verse that I couldn't do, and I set about trying to see if I could master them.

*Was this the sort of thing that John Berryman had been enjoining on you: that you should take risks and look for new ways of doing things?*

Yes, very much. And one of the things that he said he liked about me was that I seemed to be trying to write poems that were larger than I was. When he met me I was failing to achieve the poems that I was trying to write because they were beyond my ability, and he said to me once, "Whenever you find yourself writing poems you're able to write, stop and reach for poems that are larger than your ability." That's easy advice to give. He didn't always follow it, as you can see if you read all the Dream Songs; there are almost 400 and I doubt that more than 100 of them are really good. So he himself fell into the trap in middle age of imitating himself and settling for too little. But the advice is still there with me. I don't know that I've lived up to it, certainly I haven't always lived up to it, but it spurs me at least to try to give up my mannerisms and my habits and search for poetry.

*Do you find that terribly difficult, to give up the easy knack?*

I find it terribly difficult. That would be a fair estimate. It's awfully easy to go back to doing what you know you can do. And yet most of my fellow poets in the United States seem to feel that of the poets my age I have changed more than anyone else. This may be due to the fact that I live in probably greater isolation than any other American poet my age.

*Isolation from your fellow poets?*

Yes.

*Is that self-chosen or just circumstance?*

Self-chosen.

*Why do you choose to do that?*

When I don't have my eye on the immediate present—things like acceptance, publication, awards—I'm free to move into an area of real seriousness and adventuresomeness in writing. I don't want to be close to the centers of literary power and be influenced by them because I think that's very dangerous. You can fool yourself into thinking that just because people come to your readings or buy your books that you're really a terrific poet. And I hate literary shoptalk; it bores the hell out of me. Just because people treat you as though you were an important poet doesn't mean you are. In the eighteenth century there were poets of enormous reputation that no one has read in a hundred years.

*Those poets fell into that trap.*

Yes. And there are a lot of poets of my own generation that fell into that trap. I think a lot of them are sitting around like monuments fumbling their awards and taking their reputations seriously.

*There are these poets fumbling their awards.*

Yes. I think one was clearly Lowell. As a poet he got less and less interesting. He was surrounded by people who told him how terrific he was. I found that as early as his fiftieth year he was writing poetry that was technically unacceptable to him when he was my teacher. And yet somehow he faked himself out so much that he could find it acceptable when he did it. I think Robert Bly is a poet who has become incredibly boring. I don't think he was very talented to begin with, but he was able to describe snow covered with bird shit very well. But then he became a seer, as did Gary Snyder. They became very wise men, and they got up there and they told everybody in the world how they ought to live, and they still do, and like all wise men they are extraordinarily boring. They take their fame very seriously. I don't think anybody else does. They are very good as manipulators of young kids, and they travel around the universities and because they're both very good readers they're able to hypnotize the young kids. I don't know if Creeley does this. I don't think he does. He's a nice guy, a decent guy, but he's gotten to be a very dull poet. His poems have gotten to be about less and less. I think his next book will be called *Nothing*, and it will be, you know, a book without pages.

*That's a step back from minimalism, isn't it?*

Yes. Where you eliminate even the pages. His second last book will be blank pages, and his last book will be just sort of a volume of air. Duncan seems to me to be confused. The last time I saw him he said, "I'm not going to publish another book for twenty years." And I said, "Why not?" And he said, "I think I've published too many books." I agreed with him, but I wanted to say, Why don't you sit down and write a good one? I think there are some people who have been widely acclaimed who are very good, however, and remain good, although sometimes they don't write anything. A poet like Galway Kinnell. I think rather than publish bad stuff Galway would burn his poetry, and I think he does at times. Denise Levertov wrote during the Vietnam thing a lot of dull, propagandistic work, but I think during the last five or six years she's come back to writing poetry of universal theme and with all the power and technical assurance she had at her best. There are some people who are acclaimed and recognize the meaninglessness of it. All of us who receive prizes also give them. That is, I'm on the panels that give literary awards, so I know how literary awards are given and I know how much they mean. Three of us get in a room, and we say, "Do we have any friends in common that we can give this prize to and get this damn thing over quickly without having to read the books?" If you give prizes and you know how careless that awarding is and how accidental it is, it seems to me that when you get one and confuse it with genuine merit you're just an idiot—you're just a person who wants to be deluded. I've gotten a lot of awards, and I take the money and I spend it. I have a car. I have a house. I've bought three children. I have all this hair. But I don't confuse that with a literary success that has any significance. I'm glad all these things happened, but I don't confuse it with writing well.

*Writing well, for you, it seems to me has something to do*

*with maintaining through isolation or whatever other means that sense of urgency and freshness. How do you do that?*

I don't know. I'd have to say I'm very lucky. I don't control it, so that when it comes, when I write star- tlingly—about two or three weeks ago I wrote a terrific poem. I don't know where the hell it came from. It was the best poem I'd written in maybe a year. I was very tired. I'd just come back from living in New York City where I'd been for about half a year. Why this poem should invade me on this par- ticular day—I don't know. And why on that particu- lar day I remembered the man with whom the poem deals. Why I would be able to command the lan- guage to bring him forth, to embody him, I don't know. It might have something to do with the fact I didn't drink too much the night before; it might have something to do with the fact I drank just enough to dredge all that up. I can't really say. I don't understand why I write on one day and why I can't write on another. But I do understand that if I'm really drunk on Friday night I ain't gonna write on Saturday. I'm going to sit there wallowing around inside my hangover. Also, on Friday morning, if I'm selling Buicks, and I'm telling people, "The man without a Buick really ought to be ashamed of him- self," if in other words I'm misusing language in the way a Buick salesman is required to—"with this car women will really love you"—if I'm going to use lan- guage to manipulate people and lie to them, I think language and the inspiration to use language will not arrive to me. It's a very powerful superstition I have. I have this feeling that I might have been due to write a poem on Friday, but if I told a lot of terrific lies on Thursday night that inspiration will come at me and then veer off. Suddenly, somebody like Adrienne Rich will be sitting there writing poems about factory workers in Detroit and not knowing why; she will have received the inspiration I lost for having been a morally indecent human being the night before. It's a deep superstition I have that I mustn't misuse language or I won't get the chance to use it right.

*No debauching your muse, in a sense.*

That's right.

*You've spoken in the last couple minutes about being invaded by a poem as you did about your recent poem you're very pleased with.*

Yes.

*You say you don't know where inspiration comes from. What is your relationship to your creative moments?*

You used the term "muse." I think the muse is a portion of the self that largely lives asleep and that being inspired is really being totally alive. When I'm inspired I'm physically, mentally, and spiritually more me than I ordinarily am. I think the muse is a portion of the self which when it suddenly enters the conscious self makes you feel as though you were somebody else. But I think it's just you at your most. And since we are rarely ourselves at our most it does feel a little odd—and it's also delicious—and I think you learn to protract these moments to make them last as long as possible. One of the arts of writing is, I think, learning how to protract that time of inspiration so that it can include the largest possible poem that you're capable of writing at that moment. When you're a kid you get it more frequently, but you don't know what to do with it, you waste it, you blow it because you don't have the patience. "Oh, I'm inspired," and you have to run right away and write. But now I know the inspiration doesn't pass that quickly, so I walk very slowly to my chair and take my time. I like the experience, so I prolong it as much as I can.

*And how do you prolong it?*

By being confident that I will get my poem; he or she ain't gonna get away from me. I'm going to get that poem because I'm stubborn, and I know I'm inspired, so I don't have to be in a hurry. I try to take as large a view as I can, I try to begin my poem and include as much as I have experienced so that the poem can grow to encompass as much as I have lived. Sometimes I don't get away with it. I have lost the poem a couple of times. I've made it so large I can't finish the damn thing. . .

*Is that greed?*

I guess that's one way of describing it; it's also ambition. I'm not trying to take it away from somebody else, so if it's greed it's kind of a healthy greed. It's like someone trying to be as healthy as he can. If you saw me exercising violently you wouldn't say I was trying to take your health away from you. You'd say, "Go ahead, Phil, don't smoke, don't booze, do those push-ups." Also I want to share my poems with other people. I think it has to do with fulfilling myself more than anything else since it seems to me that what I'm here for is to write poems. I think it's a kind of generosity.

*And you've learned to wait patiently?*

Oh yes. I'm very patient, and I work very hard; I devote five or six mornings a week to trying to write poetry.

*And you never know when it's going to be good or when it's going to work. You just go to a certain place and sit and wait.*

Right, that's absolutely right.

*Just before we finish this interview I'd like to ask something. There was a split in American poetry, wasn't there? And to some extent this is mirrored over here or was anyway until fairly recently, I think, between the poets on the road, I suppose who stemmed from Jack Kerouac—at least he was the most notorious myth image of that sort of poet—Ginsberg, Gregory Corso, and people like that, and the academics, of whom I suppose Robert Lowell was the most famous. Where, how did you shape up between these two factions in American poetry during the sixties?*

Well, I remember when my first book came out one of the things the reviewers commented on was that they couldn't typecast me, they couldn't decide where I fitted because I was a poet of social protest, which so many of the beats were, and I was writing within traditional forms, the way the academics were, but I didn't sound like either. I certainly admired, I mean I knew personally and read and admired many of the beat poets. I was teaching, but my background was lower middle and working class. I have no respect for academia, none. I make my living there, but I think most of the people I work with are jackasses and are very jealous of me because I'm a successful writer and they're successful nothings. I never identified with either group, and I found I didn't get identified with either group. I was included in one of the anthologies that was thought of as an academic anthology. Later I was put in anthologies that were largely beat, so I wound up in both. But all that vanished after a while.

*The split?*

Yes, the split, the rift healed; people realized that it was false. There was a lot of real garbage coming out of academia; there was a lot of real garbage coming out of Haight-Ashbury in San Francisco. There was an academic poet named Wesley Trimpi who was, perhaps, the worst poet who ever lived. He wrote a poem about giving a phonograph record and some butter knives to some couple as a gift for a wedding or a wedding anniversary; it's an incredibly pompous silly poem written in very strict rhymed iambics. When you read it you said, "God, I don't want to be his fellow poet." Then there were these beat poems about people wanting to swallow Toledo, Ohio, and shit out Nineveh—just extraordinarily silly poems coming from the other camp, and you realized you couldn't evaluate either group on the basis of the crap it produced. You really had to look at somebody as good as Lowell, as good as Ginsberg, as good as Snyder. And then you saw they had a lot in common. . .

*What did they have in common?*

Language powerfully and honestly used and a knowledge of who the greatest American poet of the twentieth century was—William Carlos Williams—and that there was an American style uncluttered by the silliness that you found in the worst beat poetry or the slavish accommodation of English literary form that you found in the worst academic stuff. And there was real invention, there was real compassion for the lives that fellow Americans lived. There was really powerful thematic material and immense craft—all the good poetry had that in common. It had humanity and it had the beauty of well-wrought language. Finally whether it came out sounding like a man who'd read Milton or a man who'd read Whitman really didn't matter. Whether you found your voice in so oracular and gigantic a poet as Milton—as I think Lowell did—or whether you found it in Whitman as Allen did didn't really matter as long as you found it. They were both a part of the American poet's heritage. Wherever you went to look for the sources of inspiration as long as what you produced was honest and humane and spoke about the real lives and problems of Americans—you were going to write something that had the possibility of being important poetry. It didn't matter if you were a student of Williams, if you wound up writing about tea parties. It doesn't matter whose disciple you are if you only write about tea parties because tea parties have no real importance in a country riddled with the problems America's riddled with. What mattered to me was finding my own poetic voice or letting it find me and my ability to write about the circumstances of my own life and the lives around me; after all each of us lives a different life, and if you don't write your own poetry it isn't going to get written.

*Or indeed live your own life.*

If you live your own life you probably won't write your own poetry; you'll be too damn busy.

*Have we got any time, Phil? I just wanted to ask you . . . I know this is a very hard question to answer, but what sort of poetry, what sort of themes, what sort of direction in poetry are you interested in at the moment?*

Well, I've just finished two books that will be published next spring. People say, why don't you put them together and make one book? Well, they fall apart, and they make two books. I can talk about those, but I don't know where the hell I'm going now. The two books before these were really books of death. One was a book called *1933*, and the central poem in it was about my father's death in that year. The other book was called *The Names of the Lost*, and it was about those people whose lives are lost to us because we don't know they lived and existed and gave us something. These last two books are much more concerned with the notion of rebirth and regeneration. They're much more hopeful books, more positive. I'm not sure they're more positive. I think it's an important thing to face death and loss. I think maybe those books were born partly out of a great fear of death and loss. I no longer happen to be afraid of death; I'm not welcoming it, I don't think I'm a potential suicide. After living through those two books, I got tired of death and got much more interested in the possibility of the idea of regeneration or the possibility of violent but positive change within myself and society, and I think these books will reflect it and probably won't be as well liked as my last books because I've been typed as a very solemn and deadly poet, and some of the poems are very joyous and celebratory.

*Is this Whitman's influence? In a more direct sense, have you come back to Whitman, to that sort of celebration of life that's in Whitman?*

I think it's always been there in my poetry, and people didn't see it. I think I've been read as a much darker poet than I am. I think that as a person I'm a very merry guy, I have a good time living. I never had a problem dealing with that. My poetry has been much more concerned with those areas of my life which are problematical. One doesn't have a problem being merry, enjoying life. You know, you have a problem where fear lurks or where failure comes from. For reasons that I don't understand I didn't write out of the centers of my well-being, I seemed to write out of the centers of my woundings. I wrote so much out of them that I don't know whether they healed or whether I got bored by them. I began to shift toward the centers of my well-being; the poems of these two new books reflect that. I don't know what's in store now. I've written a lot, but I don't see a center of what will be the next book.

*Can you remember that poem, that poem that came to you a couple weeks ago, the one that came you to whole?*

No, I wish I could. I don't have it with me, and I try not to memorize my poems. I used to have a very good memory, and I have a lot of good poems in my head, but none of them are mine. I have never memorized any of my poems because I find that when I sit there to write sometimes I just start writing my old lines. [Philip Levine does not read "To Cipriano, in the Wind."]

*To Cipriano, in the Wind*

Where did your words go,
Cipriano, spoken to me 38 years
ago in the back of Peerless Cleaners,
where raised on a little wooden platform
you bowed to the hissing press
and under the glaring bulb the scars
across your shoulders—"a gift
of my country"—gleamed like old wood.
"*Dignidad,*" you said into my boy's
wide eyes, "without is no riches."
And Ferrente, the dapper Sicilian
coatmaker, laughed. What could
a pants presser know of dignity?
That was the winter of '41, it
would take my brother off to war,
where you had come from, it would
bring great snowfalls, graying
in the streets, and the news of death
racing through the halls of my school.
I was growing. Soon I would be
your height, and you'd tell me
eye to eye, "Some day the world
is ours, some day you will see."
And your eyes burned in your fine
white face until I thought you
would burn. That was the winter
of '41, Bataan would fall
to the Japanese and Sam Baghosian
would make the long march
with bayonet wounds in both legs,
and somehow in spite of burning acids

splashed across his chest and the acids
of his own anger rising toward his heart
he would return to us and eat
the stale bread of victory. Cipriano,
do you remember what followed
the worst snow? It rained all night
and in the dawn the streets gleamed,
and within a week wild phlox leaped
in the open fields. I told you
our word for it, "Spring," and you said,
"Spring, spring, it always come after."
Soon the Germans rolled east
into Russia and my cousins died. I
walked alone in the warm spring winds
of evening and said, "Dignity." I said
your words, Cipriano, into the winds.
I said, "Someday this will all be ours."
Come back, Cipriano Mera, step
out of the wind and dressed in the robe
of your pain tell me again that this
world will be ours. Enter my dreams
or my life, Cipriano, come back
out of the wind.

*The old danger again. . .*

Yes, but I won't sit there and write Dylan Thomas, I
won't just write, "The force that through the green
fuse drives the flower. . ." Also I find if I memorize
my poems that when I give a poetry reading I'm
much more boring because there aren't any sur-
prises. When I read I try to read poems I haven't
read recently; I keep jumping around in my work,
one book one night, another book the next, and so
on; just so there are lots of surprises for me because
this excites me and I read better. If I don't know
where the poem is going I say to myself, "Gee, that's

pretty good. Look what I did! I wish I could write that well tomorrow!"

*Just for the record who is going to publish these two new books?*

Atheneum.

*Atheneum, right, and what are their names?*

7 *Years from Somewhere* and *Ashes.*

Ashes, *right. Phil, I've enjoyed this enormously, talking with you.*

Thank you. It's been a lot of fun.

# Interview with David Remnick

Sausalito, California, Winter, 1978

*The poem "The Children's Crusade" from* They Feed They Lion *is an atypical poem for you because its whole conception is far more—well, allegorical.*

It's about the late sixties and those members of my generation and especially of my profession who thought they ought to tell the children the final truths about the nature of everything, those guru types, Leary and all the little seers that I resent enormously. The kids turn on this man in the poem and destroy him. I'm with the kids. Their savagery delights me. [Philip Levine reads "The Children's Crusade."]

### The Children's Crusade

Crossbow wanted a child,
a little schoolboy with a red hole
in his brow

like the President. He excited
everyone. They made a brilliant
pair of angel's wings from Kaiser foil

and posterboard, they made a little
tufted box. They would cross his arms
on a single burning peony.

They'd get a glossy Testament,
a blanket tucked in
deep around the sides.

He wanted the little boy who skipped
all the way to school. Eve shook
her red head, and the silver

ignition keys hooked in her
pierced ears chirped. "No, No,"
he was going to be

her lover friend. She wanted
someone like Daddy. Archangel said,
"Daddy."

They took stations.
The night hollered through
the branches and the long grass

like a burned TV.
They bit their hands and waited
Daddy's car closed.

Everything went quiet and they
had to still their heads like they'd learned
when the bedroom door opened.

After they stabbed him down,
Eve came out from
the shadows. She pulled his beard

but only a little came loose.
She stood so tall in mother's shoes,
and with blue and green chalk

on her lids and cheeks,
he never
knew her. He licked his lips

like when he said important
things, and spread his arms
and made his eyes make tears,

he wanted to talk, he wanted
to help them all, but she just pushed
the knife between his teeth.

When he stopped, they tried
to finish. The box was way too small
and he was too heavy.

So they giggled. When they smelled
what he'd done, they giggled
more. A Daddy going ka ka!

They rolled him over and tore
rags of skin from the eucalyptus
and hid him forever.

Now they ran. The shadows
were all gone, and the air
growing as soft as stone

underwater. Underwater or in moonlight,
the hills rose above the earth,
and they ran shedding their caps and bells,

the little silent bells
they wore at wrist and ankle,
they threw away their names and their no-names.

They cast their knives on the absent waters
and their long bamboo spears.
"Goodbye, rusty can opener, Goodbye!"

The houses were snapping.
It was over and they ran. Never
to wait! Now they were free.

It's a hard poem to defend because there is so much hostility and violence in it, but I think that violence is what adults have taught children. It's also a turnabout on the historical Children's Crusade, where the adults sent the kids off on this ridiculous quest and turned them into slaves, concubines, and corpses. In this poem Daddy is going to exercise his Godhead, but the kids are on to him. I don't mind young people lying because it seems to me that's part of the nature of being young; you don't know the truth, or you do and you try to hide it. What I saw and hated was older people lying to themselves and to young kids. There's a point when if you don't level with young kids you're betraying them. What I saw were older people who were unwilling or psychologically unable to accept the disapproval of young people. As a teacher I think you should be honest and let the kids know what you stand for, and if they don't want it, they don't take it.

*You've said elsewhere that you consider yourself to be a romantic poet. What do you really mean by that?*

Too often we think a romantic poet is one obsessed with the self. I think that's irrelevant. I wouldn't call Sylvia Plath a romantic poet even though she writes so much about herself. It seems to me that the inferences you make after reading her are that people are largely demented and evil and need strong governance. It's strange that a woman who could react so violently against concentration camps winds up almost suggesting they have a function, that a lot of people belong in them or in mental institutions, which are just more sophisticated forms of camps. If the self that is portrayed in poems is violent and dangerous, the reader's only sensible reaction is to think, "let's be careful, perhaps some people should be enchained." Whatever beauty I see in the natural world, whatever spirit I think is immanent in it, I feel is also there in people who are themselves part of the natural world. I remember as a student when my teachers would use the terms "classic" and "romantic," I would ask, "Why isn't man part of the natural world? He got on this planet like everything else." I never got a decent answer.

*Was Judaism influential early on for you?*

I don't think so. I thought it was a religion that preached exclusiveness.

*In the marital sense?*

In every sense. I'm talking about the culture more than the faith. I was told that people who weren't Jewish hated me, and I ought to hate them, and no matter how I kidded myself sooner or later they'd get me. I was supposed to be somehow superior to them either because I did let them get me or I didn't—I could have my choice. I found the Old Testament a powerful book, but again there was the exclusiveness and the unforgiving nature of God. I see people who are able to forgive. I don't think God would be worse than his creations.

*Were you interested in poetry or fiction when you began?*

I began by wanting to write fiction.

*What kind did you write?*

Mediocre, I would say.

*I spoke with Michael Harper, a poet you've advised in the past. He is very interested in sorting out his African and American pasts in his poems. Is your European and Jewish past a major concern?*

It may be. Once I was reading in a place in Wisconsin, and an older man asked me to read certain poems, one of which was "Baby Villon," which is about an Algerian prizefighter. Afterward the man introduced himself; he was Abe Chapman, and he was doing an anthology of Jewish-American writing. To him "Baby Villon" was a Jewish poem. I saw what he meant: it is a celebration of courage and integrity and the difficulty of life wherever it takes place. We were a people scattered all over the world who knew what it was to be scattered all over the world. We knew what it was to be underdogs and to survive in the face of the enmity and disrespect of others. We knew we were a noble people no matter what anyone told us to the contrary. Our great cultural heritage was that we could feel the suffering of any people and know that any people was as good as any other.

*Charles Wright explained to me that he writes in a kind of opposite way from you. His writing is very fragmented, yours is very narrative. You're not always telling a story, but usually there is some kind of narrative line from which everything takes off. Do you think narratively? Do you tell stories usually?*

That's one of the ways my mind works. I've always told stories, and I grew up with people who were wonderful storytellers. I think the most exciting poems are in some way narrative. I find Charles's poetry often arbitrary in the way it's structured. He'll say, "I've got this book of forty poems and each is sixteen lines or under, and there has to be one poem that is one line long." He showed me the book, and I said, "The one liner stinks," and he said, "I know, but I have to have it." To me that's ridiculous; something can trigger your imagination, but to be loyal to such an arbitrary structure seems nuts. I'm no longer loyal to any notion of structure. That's the biggest difference between our poetry. I think he's right, though, in the sense that there is often a need for a precise scheme for a poem, and he knows better than I what he needs. I have a much greater trust of the irrational; maybe it's because I'm more rational.

*Do you ever do automatic writing?*

I probably do it all the time, but I never think I do. I think I'm in complete command.

*Do you write first drafts quickly?*

Yes, I revise very quickly too. Say a poem is forty lines long; I can write the first draft—when I'm hot—in twenty minutes, and two hours later I've gone through six drastic revisions and the poem is finished.

*Gary Snyder has said that he never begins to write until he has the poem memorized, and then he begins.*

Not me. Usually for me the act of writing is the act of discovery. I'll sit down with certain images, sometimes I'll almost have a tune, and there is an emotional urgency pressing me. Then I might discover what I'm being pressed toward. If I had the whole poem memorized I might not even write it down.

*Do you often start with warm-up lines? Maybe you don't even know they're warm-up lines until you've discarded them and have begun what really is to be the poem?*

It's very rare for me not to do what you just described. I sort of write through a conventional me, and then there's a point where I might break into something fresh, and I'll start from there and throw the rest away.

*What are the conditions you write under? Do you need quiet?*

I work with a pen and paper and need quiet. That's about all. It doesn't matter where I am. I can work with another person in the same room as long as I'm not looking at that person. If my wife were over there and she were sewing or whatever, I could face away from her and work. I grew up as a writer with kids in the house and very little money, so I didn't have a room which was my own to write in.

*Have you ever tried drugs along with writing? Or are there any externals that enter into your writing conditions?*

Physical well-being. I rarely write when I'm sick or hung over. I've never written except in sobriety.

*Never tried it?*

When I was very young. It was bullshit.

*Do you think as many poems were written in drug states as poets claim?*

I disbelieve that as many came out of drugs as their authors say, but I'm sure some did. I feel that poets lie about what they do. In a letter Keats will tell his brother he ripped off a poem one morning, but we have the manuscripts, and it took him eighty-two drafts. I don't know if people have lied about drugs. If drugs got me into poetry, I'd take drugs. What I've found is that certain drugs hurt my memory, and since for me so much of my material is my memory, I have to be careful. I found hallucinogens boring. Emotionally and intellectually nothing much was going on. I didn't feel that the door and I were suddenly part of God. I just thought the door was moving around, being a little more aggressive than usual. I smoked dope all the time when I was a kid and had no idea God was hiding in it.

*You didn't know you were a junior mystic?*

That's right. I just thought it was a way of fucking off at work.

*One of the catch phrases that is always being thrust upon younger poets is the exhortation to "find your own voice." What does that mean?*

Most good poets have a recognizable way of saying things. You don't have to have seen the poem before to say this is Berryman or Lowell or Levertov. I never tell young poets to find their own voice because I don't think that's how voice comes to us.

Once a poet discovers what his material is, his voice will come to him. The best thing is to practice good writing until you've got something urgent to say, so urgent it has to be said. When it's got to be said, you'll say it in your own voice. I don't think anyone ever found his own voice, it found him.

*Do you have some positive advice for younger poets?*

People should write what they're interested in writing. First I think one must realize that he or she has his whole lifetime to become a poet. To be in a hurry to write a masterpiece is nuts. Very few young people have written masterpieces. Sure a genius comes along once in a while. But Rimbaud doesn't have to ask his creative writing teacher anything; he's already thrown his creative writing teacher through the window. You don't find people like that in creative writing classes, so you don't have to concern yourself with them. If students come to an older person like me and they are interested in writing, I tell them to try writing as many different things as they can. You learn a lot by failing. Don't be afraid to fail. What the fear of failing eventuates in is the fear of beginning. If you're writing ten or twelve good poems a year you're writing ten or twelve more good ones than anyone else, since only about two get written in the country each year.

*Michael Harper also said about you that you were one of the few white poets who could take on a black voice without being condescending. He spoke of the poem "They Feed They Lion" specifically.*

That was generous of Michael. We're friends.

*You've written in a very compressed short line for a long time. Occasionally there are spasms of length, but usually it's a short trimeter line. Why have you stayed with that, and where does it come from?*

I think I developed that line from my favorite line, which is Yeats's trimeter line. I think it comes from an attempt to find a free verse equivalent. He can use it in a song-like way or mold it into long paragraphs of terrific rhythmic power. I was very early awed by the way he could keep the form and let the syntax fall across it in constantly varying ways, the way certain sixteenth-century poets could with pentameter. The short line appeals to me because I think it's easier to make long statements that accumulate great power in short lines. You can flow line after line, and the breaks become less significant because there are so many of them, and they build to great power.

*What do you mean when you say you're an anarchist?*

I mean I think I'm an anarchist.

*Could you explain the difference between anarchism and the new right-wing libertarianism of Ayn Rand and economists like Greenspan and Milton Friedman? They go so far as to say that if they want to set up a potentially exploitive enterprise it's their business. That's their version of unbridled individual liberty.*

If you're going to allow people to make all the important choices about their lives you're going to be relying on them to make decent choices. If people are going to make unwise and disgusting choices that tyrannize their brothers and sisters, then they have violated a profound anarchist tenet: you don't tyrannize other people. In accepting your own freedom you have to grant others theirs. One basis of anarchism is the appalling confidence people will act decently.

*What is your attitude toward politics as subject matter in your own poems? What place does it hold?*

Recently a woman asked me a question that answered itself. She said, "Do you feel in your poetry that the people in your poems are there to be cherished because the world hasn't cherished them?" She noted how many people appeared in my poems.

*An early poem, "Animals Are Passing from Our Lives," seems almost to me to be an emblem of your attitude, a hard-nosed reverence for the individual and an appreciation of that quality in others, even in a lowly pig.*

That poem celebrates the quality of digging in your heels. Even the little pig will not do things the way people expect him to. He's going to die his own way. There's a lot of abuse being heaped on the culture that's taking him to his death. Even though he knows he's dying for an appalling society, he's not going to beg for his life. They're not going to make a pig out of him. They call him a pig, they treat him like a pig, they'll kill him like a pig, but he's going to act with more dignity than a human being.

> *Animals Are Passing from Our Lives*
>
> It's wonderful how I jog
> on four honed-down ivory toes

my massive buttocks slipping
like oiled parts with each light step.

I'm to market. I can smell
the sour, grooved block, I can smell
the blade that opens the hole
and the pudgy white fingers

that shake out the intestines
like a hankie. In my dreams
the snouts drool on the marble,
suffering children, suffering flies,

suffering the consumers
who won't meet their steady eyes
for fear they could see. The boy
who drives me along believes

that any moment I'll fall
on my side and drum my toes
like a typewriter or squeal
and shit like a new housewife

discovering television,
or that I'll turn like a beast
cleverly to hook his teeth
with my teeth. No. Not this pig.

*You talked earlier about your decision not to serve in the
Korean War, and in one of your new books,* 7 Years from
Somewhere, *there's a poem, "Dawn, 1952," that explicitly
deals with that. Is it difficult to write about something so
clearly autobiographical?*

In this case it must have been. The experience took
place when I was twenty-five, and I wrote the poem
when I was fifty. There's only one earlier poem that
mentions it. In the poem "And the Trains Go On,"
in *The Names of the Lost,* I wrote that I'm "on the run

from a war no one can win." That's not really saying I was a draft dodger in the Korean War.

*How did you get out of the service?*

I refused to go. I was lucky and wasn't prosecuted.

*Why not?*

Well, I didn't ask to be prosecuted, so you'd have to ask them why not. If you looked at newspapers printed during World War II and the Korean War I doubt you'd find much reference to draft resistance.

*Why do you think Americans write so much weak political poetry?*

Because it's written under the wrong sense of obligation. I think good poems demand to be written from inside the poet. What I think happens with most political poems is that poets are in certain situations and think a poem is needed, and they are obliged to sit down and write it, and they produce crap.

*What if one chooses to use place names and trademarks of the era? Is it possible to use them and write something that isn't quickly dated.*

*War and Peace* isn't dated because there are lives you believe in caught up in those struggles. Wilfred Owen isn't dated because you believe he's there. And while Hardy wasn't there, he has an imagination that's so powerful, he could put you there. Great talents can overcome the limitations of the political poem. During the Vietnam war poets felt real disgust at being American or at being alive and well while others were burning to death, but we didn't know how to write about it.

*You mentioned before that you often write quickly. How long are you able to stick with a particular problematic poem?*

Not long enough. Two or three months. One of the poems I've recently done is called "The Poem Following Me." I first wrote it in 1965, but I threw it away. I did it again in 1968 and 1974, but they were no better. And now again I did it this past fall. This poem is haunting me, demanding to be written. There are some poems I might even go back and change, and I seldom do that. I'd like to shorten the poem "1933." I think I could make it more precise and moving; I think I published it too quickly.

*One additional question. To a certain extent you continue writing in a similar voice and about similar subjects. Are there any changes or new directions you envision for yourself in the near future?*

Yes, but I can't describe them. I don't understand what's happening to me.

# Interview with Tad Prozewicz

Fresno, California, Spring, 1979

It is a late March morning of 1979. Levine is seated in the back room of his house on Van Ness Blvd. in Fresno, which is a beautiful tree-lined street of large lots and handsome homes. His home is the oldest and smallest on the entire street. It's 12:30 P.M. when we begin, but he is still in his bathrobe and seems in no hurry to do anything. From the back window we can see dark clouds scudding overhead, and occasionally there is a short downpour. This room, his study, is an incredible mess: there are stacks of paper and books everywhere, there is a small bed a foot deep in books and drafts of poems, the large homemade desk is a sea of pens, scribbled notes, opened and unopened letters. The walls are decorated with the mementos of his loyalties. The most conspicuous thing above his desk is a large black and white drawing which he refers to as "The Rabbi of Auschwitz," drawn by his friend the Italian anarchist painter Flavio Costantini. On its right is an old photo in sepia of his family, his mother stands in the rear, his older brother sits majestically in a chair, and the five-year-old Philip and his twin, Edward, are at his knees. To the left are two photos, one of several poets—Nancy Willard and Mark Strand are recognizable along with a younger Levine—and below it is a photo of a man he worked with twenty or more years ago in Detroit. On the far side of the window is a Walker Evans photo of a Pennsylvania store front, next to it a grainy shot of his hero Buenaventura Durruti while in exile in Brussels, and next to it an original Robert Capa of Spanish Republican soldiers bundled in rags and waiting for chow. Near the door is a small picture taken by Levine of the grave of Durruti in the great cemetery of Barcelona. Levine seems very comfortable in these surroundings and sips at a cup of mint tea.

*You must be sick of interviews.*

Not as sick as the people who have to read them, but then I suppose no one has to read them.

*Are you asked the same questions over and over?*

No. But what's worse is I give the same answers over and over, even when the questions are different. I recall two very nice young men from Davis who interviewed me; they tried for hours to get the events of my life straight, and in truth I was unable or unwilling to clarify much. I think I prefer to keep my private life private. Besides I don't find my personal life very interesting. Remember Keats's remark about the poet being the least poetical of beings? It's dull enough to have to live my life, but it's hopeless to have to describe it. I think that's why I invent certain events.

*Which ones?*

You find out. I try to be honest about most things, especially the things that matter, but there are other things I'd rather have fun with. At Vassar a young woman from the college paper asked me to talk about the suffering of the poor young poet. I said I knew nothing about any of that. I came from a rich family. She said she thought I was from Detroit and had been a factory worker. I said, yes, I was from Detroit, but my family had been very rich. My grandfather invented the automobile, but he called it a Ford because he felt the world wasn't ready for a Levine.

*Did she know you were joking?*

I would think she'd have to, but she didn't let on. Listen, I'll tell you a nuttier one. A woman called and offered me a hundred dollars to read in San Francisco. I said, "OK, but only for dogs and cats." "What?" she said. I said, "I charge five hundred dollars to read for people, but I'm interested in how pets respond to poetry. They hear humans speaking all the time, and I'm curious if they can tell the difference between ordinary speech and poetry." "Can't a few people be there too?" "No," I said, "five hundred for people, one hundred for household pets. I can only give so many readings a year, and I want to earn the most for them." So she said, "I don't see the difference. You're reading anyway, whether to dogs and cats or to people." She's dead serious about this. I said, "Well, the dogs and cats don't tell anyone how long you read or how much you gave it."

*Did she think you were crazy?*

She should have, but I'm not sure she did. She kept trying to make sense out of it. In *A Moveable Feast* Hemingway makes a big thing about what a liar Ford Madox Ford was. I have the feeling Ford invented all sorts of trivial crap but was honest about the things that mattered. I just get that sense from his great fiction; whereas Hemingway could tell you to the nearest hundred how many different women he went to bed with, but he hadn't the faintest idea of who he was or why. I think he was completely seduced by his own pose, the way Mailer is now, and like Mailer I think he became a less and less attractive person and less interesting as a writer. I no longer care what Mailer thinks about much of anything, which is sad because the guy had immense talent as a writer and brilliance and courage as a sort of spiritual weathervane. But Norman on prizefighting is in the same league with such lightweights as Plimpton and Cosell. Not one of them can even see a fight much less see the significance of one.

*What do you mean, they can't see a fight?*

Well, you have to know what to look for. It's like anything else, you've got to train yourself to perceive it. It's like poetry reading or bird watching.

*Can you see a fight?*

Yeah, as long as I'm not in it.

*And the significance?*

It's enormous for the fighters. Money, fame, movies for the winner or broken bones, a broken heart, loss, loneliness. The closer you get the more awful it is, and some of the great ones wound up with no money, no body, and no brains—Johnny Bratton, Ezzard Charles, Eddie Machen. It's a brutal sport, a cruel diversion. It's disgusting.

*Is it more significant than the academic world?*

No. It's more dramatic and interesting. The academic world touches millions of us who go through it, and then there are the thousands who remain in it until they turn into bookends or erasers or split infinitives.

*Are you one of them?*

Probably. I don't like to see myself that way, but I've spent about fifteen of the last twenty-three years teaching somewhere or other. I don't find academia very congenial. I had a very hard time as a student. I was working for a living, and on the job I was treated as a man, but in the classroom I was often treated as a boy, and I bridled at that. I had to tell one teacher to treat me as an equal or I'd unwind his clock.

*What did he do?*

He did his best to address me as an equal. He didn't have much experience treating people as equals, so he didn't do it very well, but I gave him an A for effort. I should add that in a lot of academic situations I've been treated very well, at Fresno, Columbia, Vassar, Montana, Indiana. But at Princeton, Cincinnati, Stanford, Goddard I didn't eat for fear of the mess I'd make. There were a lot of places where one day was one too many, and others where people were so wonderful to me I didn't want to leave. I make a lot of easy generalizations about academia, but in fact there are very few "ivory towers" in the United States. Princeton is one. It has a Georgian Greyhound bus station that is less than 100 miles but is 427 light years from New York City. And a school can be a dump, like Cincinnati, and shit on you.

*Are you pleased you've spent so many years teaching?*

I doubt it. I don't know. It beats working. But it's given my poetry very little, or perhaps I should say it's given me very little I could transform into poetry. Detroit gave me a great deal, but it gives others nothing. But the academic world may be like certain places, like Cincinnati or Columbus or Akron, no one can make poetry out of them.

*Why do you live in Fresno?*

Why not? You've got to live somewhere. And I love this house. My wife loves it. Look how beautiful she's made it—I don't mean this room, she never comes in here, you're only the second person to come in here. The first disappeared. Look at that beautiful garden out there, look at those orange trees.

*And the school, Fresno State, what do you think of it?*

The school stinks. It's determined not to do the job it

might do, educate the people of this valley so they could make meaningful choices about how they live. When in the late sixties it became for a short time an effective place, and the blacks and Chicanos were learning what their real function in this culture was, the powers that be fired the entire Black Studies faculty and La Raza faculty, just like that. No reason. It's been downhill since then.

*Yet you've had some amazing students.*

Yes, Larry Levis, David St. John, Sherley Williams, Herb Scott, Glover Davis, Luis Salinas, Steve Jamison, Roberta Spear, Leonard Adame, Greg Pape, Lance Patigian, and more. Bob Jones, Gary Soto, Dennis Saleh, Dewayne Rail.

*Why in a place like this?*

I don't know. We never recruited them.

*Could it be you?*

It could be. But it's hard to believe one teacher could make such a difference. Pete Everwine and Hanzlicek also taught a lot of these people. I get most of the credit because I'm better known.

*I've heard you're going to leave.*

So have I.

*Is that all you have to say about it?*

I don't know the future. I don't teach as much as I

used to. My kids are all grown up, and I don't need as much money. And my poetry and my readings make a lot more money than they used to.

*Speaking of your children, did you ever think there was a conflict between being a father and being a poet?*

Yes, in my head I was sure this would be an enormous problem, just as I thought being an industrial worker would stop me from writing. Neither did. I relived much of my childhood and growing up as my kids went through those experiences, and I wrote about them. And of course my poems are full of the people I met as a factory worker back in Detroit and they're full of the city itself, the city as it was then.

I always thought I was a lousy father, and then one day not long ago—maybe a year or so ago—I saw that all three of my sons were gutsy and independent as hell. My "baby" Teddy lives in Detroit, makes a lot of bread, is gentle and strong as a horse, and takes shit from no one. Mark is twenty-seven and trying his best to make it as a sculptor in New York City. John is a carpenter here in California.

*But you thought you were a lousy father?*

Yeah. I said this to my wife, and she said, bullshit! You were terrific. You'd play games with them for hours every night, and you did it because you loved it. And you told them wild stories every night. So they didn't have color TV, they had your sagas. Maybe she's right, I thought. And maybe having a father who's still in his pajamas at 3 P.M. slaving at a poem is a good thing. It's not your standard image of the father, but it's a guy who's gonna do what he wants to do no matter what. And maybe that's why they're unafraid of the world, so much less afraid, I think, than I was at their age.

*What's ahead?*

The future. I'm not the Delphic oracle. You're gonna fuck your mother and kill your father.

*Thanks. Do you like being famous?*

I'll let you know when I'm famous.

*What do you think of your generation of poets?*

We've gone through some strange times, some strange changes, but I think we'll make a real contribution. We're not the Frost, Stevens, Eliot, Williams, Pound group, but we're OK.

*Who are we?*

I'll forget some. Kinnell, Jim Wright, Stafford, Jane Cooper, Plath, Gerry Stern, Ginsberg, Justice, Hecht, Merrill, Dickey, Bly, Snyder, Rich, Ashbery, Creeley, Sexton, Merwin, and the ones I forgot. Everwine, Denise.

*How good are they?*

I forgot Levine.

*How good are you, all of you?*

You're gonna fuck your aunt and marry your uncle.

*Are you as good as the others or better?*

John Haines, who I forgot, once told me he liked me but he was sorry he didn't like the book *They Feed They Lion.* I told him to read it again. It's a good book. I saw him a year later and he agreed. Richard Hugo, Madeline De Frees, Don Hall. Nice names. Galway and Justice have the best names. I get Philip Levine. Is that fair? In my whole life the guy who looked the most like a poet was the Irish poet Richard Murphy, and he writes like a dog with eight paws. I forgot Finkel, Etheridge Knight, John Engels, LeRoi Jones, Art Rimbaud. Jesus Christ, it's raining like mad. Do you think the rain will hurt the snails?

*Why don't you write criticism?*

Why don't you? I'm a poet. If we need that shit, you spend your time writing it. I'm a writer and if I'm going to do it I'm going to try to do it well, and it'll take time away from my real work. I was teaching at Princeton a while back with Stan Plumly, who is a hell of a poet, and he was working on this big thing for *American Poetry Review,* a critical piece. It came out, it was intelligent, it was profound at times, but I didn't need it. I wonder if even the people he wrote about needed it. The other day I got a piece from *Critical Inquiry* from the University of Chicago. It was by Peter Viereck and titled "Strict Form in Poetry: Would Jacob Wrestle with a Flabby Angel?" Viereck wanted me to write a response to its main point, that poetry without strict form and rhyme is not challenging enough for a real talent. Now how the hell would Viereck know? He never wrote a decent poem with or without rhyme. But the title interests me. I thought about it for some time. Of course Jacob would fight for his life—he was a proud Jew. I once fought with an angel, or so I believe, and I gave it everything I had and still got destroyed. Wow! Did that cat throw me around. I was sure I was going to die, but I held on with all the energy I had, and here I am, a wiser man.

*Really?*

Yes. I had that thumping coming. I'd forgotten that we aren't all lucky or tough, and those of us who are have to love those of us who aren't and look out for them. After that beating I was neither lucky or tough for some years, and a lot of people kept me alive. There were some who didn't, who saw I was down and creamed me while they had the chance, but the others kept me going. I was scared, oh was I, but my true beloveds kept me alive, and I'm wiser now, and that may be why the angels are elsewhere.

*Where?*

They may get you tonight when you're fucking your nephew and marrying your niece.

*What do you think of all these liberation movements poetry gets involved in?*

Well, people get involved in them. They see them as relevant, important to their lives, so I think it's a good thing that poetry gets involved in them too.

*Do you think they're valid?*

Of course. If you're black and you can't get a decent job, and you look around and most of the other people waiting for unemployment checks are also black, you're gonna say, hey, we want a fair shake. If you belong to a minority group that's insulted and injured I think it's natural to identify with that group, blacks, native Americans, hillbillies in Chicago, Okies in California, gays, Chicanos, women. Though women aren't a minority they're certainly insulted and injured. The country owes them a much better chance for life.

*So you agree with Adrienne Rich?*

She used to be a friend. She'd come to my house and say it was lovely to see two people, Fran and me, in love for so long. She even said that in public once when I'd introduced her at a reading, and she kissed me in front of 500 people, mainly women, and then went on to tell the women that we, the men, were all apes. The last time I called her I did so because a mutual friend said she was depressed and I might cheer her up. So I phoned her and got through her body guards, and she said, "Yes?" And I said, "Hello, Adrienne, this is Phil." She said, "Phil?" "Yeah, Phil Levine." "What do you want?" I should have said, "I want some pussy," because she was using a voice Mussolini would have used to a street cleaner. Instead I think I said, "Nice to talk to you." I haven't given up on her—I'm sure she'll be delighted to hear that—she's got plenty of brains and heart. She'll come back. Women are insulted and injured. So are industrial workers. That doesn't mean every worker should throw a bomb into a bank or a jewelry store. But it does mean that that's what you want to do so badly it kills you. At twenty I wanted to kill hundreds of rich, superior, disdainful motherfuckers. Oh, how they rode above it all.

*You don't anymore?*

No. I don't think I want to kill anyone. First, money doesn't have to make you an asshole. It just usually does. But I've met people born of money who had soul, and I've met poor people who were as cold as ice. It's not as easy as I once thought. And I don't want to be a killer. There are hateful people who are just begging for it. I'd like to see the whole Nixon clan working for the rest of their lives in children's hospitals in Vietnam attending to the wounds they inflicted in the name of the free world.

*Did you get involved in the antiwar thing?*

Yep.

*No more to say?*

I could say I stopped the war with my little poems, I turned this country right around and now it's beautiful. But I won't.

*What about the poems you wrote then?*

Will you look at that rain.

*Are you surprised how much your work has changed?*

No, I don't think it's changed as much as I have. I'm still writing about the same people, plus some others,

I'm still telling my little stories, trying to capture the places I dig, the people, get them down on paper. I'm still obsessed with the crazy thing we all make up together.

*What thing?*

Oh, you know, the thing that comes into being because we touch each others' lives and become part of each other. That I'm still a young man in Detroit, where my son is also now a young man, and I'm a woman in California, a guy wandering the roads of Alabama and Georgia looking for a welcome, and I'm the man or woman who could welcome me. All our lives we're taught we're different, and slowly we find out otherwise. In my imagination—and because I trust my imagination, I'd have to say "in fact"—I'm many people, some dead, some living, and that's still what I want to capture in my poetry.

*You think it's an illusion, that we're different?*

Yes. I think most of what we're taught are simply illusions. I start school when I'm five, and what's the first thing I'm taught? I am important, I'm a citizen of the United States. I could be the president because this is like no other country. Well, first I couldn't be the president for twenty reasons. Then this country is like the others. And finally the United States is an illusion. Some jackoff comes here and plants a flag of a European nation and says, "I claim this in the name of the King of Dogs." There were people here, and they didn't own the land. The land owned them. No one owns the land. The land was here before we were. All this ownership is paper, lies, bullshit. We were put on this earth to be happy, to share our lives with all that's here. We should try to leave the place in a little better shape than when we found it. We're here to take care of it, not to drain and exhaust it.

*Does this mean you have trouble being a good citizen?*

No. I'm a good citizen. I love America, the place, the people. Just because I wouldn't obey my government and go kill gooks doesn't mean I'm not a valuable person.

*What's your value?*

More than you've got. You're too tall for me. Besides I'm not partial to beards.

*You had one yourself for years.*

True, but I didn't make love to myself. For a while I wanted to look old. I was tired of love, maybe I was scared of new love, maybe I was scared of all the possibilities that were still available, so I crawled inside this wise rabbi costume and waited for my hair to turn white.

*What happened?*

I began, of a sudden, as the poet says, to feel younger, to look younger, not to care about all the scary possibilities. I knew that I would be a man at least this once. I thought, let's go for it all. See what you can get out of it, see what you can put into it. I was already a man, I was a holy creature without being a rabbi. In a profound way I trusted myself. I shaved the beard, I got a new tailor, I said, "Levine, take care of yourself, drink less, live more. It's now or never."

*And?*

It's now. I'm fine.

*And your poetry, does it reflect this?*

I think so. I think it's all there if you look closely. Hayden Carruth digs my poetry, and he's a very close reader. In one recent piece he said I was the poet of desolation, of a world without solace. He may be right. Calvin Bedient thinks I'm a romantic poet. Joyce Carol Oates thinks I'm a visionary. Could be. I'm not sure what my vision is, but maybe none of the visionary poets were that sure of what they were about. I'm just happy that people get something of value from my work. God knows, Joyce and Hayden have given me a great deal from their work; I'm honored to give them something back.

*Do you have any idea where your work will go?*

Not really. I discover it day by day. I'd be surprised if I got myself into a mammoth poem, especially if it turned out to be a long sequence of poems. Most of those things bore me. I'm sorry Pound spent so much of his creative life on the Cantos, and I think Berryman should have quit after the first seventy-seven Dream Songs. I think those long sequences are a way of avoiding the truth.

*Which is?*

That a poem is not a gimmick, a formula, and each poem is a new beginning, and often—as Keats knew as a boy wonder—you have to sit with your wings furled and wait for the moment to fly. That can be awfully tough.

*I notice you quote Keats a lot.*

A lot more than he quotes me.

*Why?*

Because I read him, and he didn't read me. Because he was a little miracle. I had a kid at Vassar ask me how anyone twenty-four could know so much. I reminded her that Keats didn't have an adolescence. When you've got no money and you've got responsibilities you grow up in a hurry. In his teens he was trying to raise his two brothers and his sister and train himself to be a surgeon and still write poetry. That Vassar girl might be forty before she saw as much of life as he saw at twenty-four. Talk about his vision, read the letter about the world as a "vale of soul-making." How hard he tried to make some decent meaning out of the terrible world he inherited. The man who emerges in his letters may be a kid in years but he's a giant in his soul.

*What do you think of his theory of negative capability?*

I think it's a remarkably accurate description of how I live: in the midst of uncertainties, doubts, half-truths, confusion I try to write poems, I try to make decisions. I try to lead the best life I can. In my book *1933* I have a poem called "At the Fillmore" which is about two young people at a rock concert who are blinded by light and deafened by noise and in spite of that make the choice to try to love each other, and they accept all the consequences, and since they've lost before they know how heavy the consequences can be. I love those people because they're not afraid to live life as it must be lived, as it's given us to live.

*You think we're in the dark?*

Yes, but it's light enough.

*What does that mean?*

It means you should read Keats.

*Anyone else?*

Of course. Do you know Alun Lewis?

*No.*

Go stand in the corner. Edward Thomas? Thomas Nashe?

*No.*

I'll break your pencils. One poet leads you to another, and you have a lifetime to read. Don't feel bad, you've got the time to read them all. Last year I was teaching at Columbia, and one student accused another of writing like Tess Gallagher, and the accused admitted her theft. I said, "You cretins. Don't steal from Tess. She's fine, but she's just finding her way. Steal from Rilke, Wordsworth, Hardy, Stevens, Milosz, Owen, Hopkins, Whitman. Steal diamonds, not pebbles." Then I had to show them the jewels. But they were a wonderful class. I really got to love them. I think I helped some of them.

*How?*

The way you help anyone. By taking him or her seriously. They pawned off the "no talents" on me. I was just there for a semester, so they said, "Work with these zeroes." But they were not zeroes. They were real people, not kids, adults, and gifted adults. When I started to listen to their poems and make demands on them, they came through. At first the class hated me because I was sort of brutal with mediocre poems and I spent too much time on dead poets, but after a while we all got used to each other and something lovely took place—at least for me.

*Something lovely?*

Yes. It can be intoxicating to be of real use to other people. I have enormous energy and I am very experienced in the ways of helping poets and poems, and when I get a chance and my brain is ON, it's a fantastic experience. I know I'm not being modest right now, but I think I'm being truthful. I'm not always any good, but one hot day makes up for five cold ones.

*Is that the way you live?*

I don't live any way. When I get out of bed in the

morning I don't have a script. I invent my life every day, except for the lazy days when I let the weather call the shots. I'm not afraid to fail. I've failed at so many things, I suppose damn near everything, and it's not tragic. I may finally be a total flop as a poet. The year after I die someone will say, "That guy Levine spent fifty years trying to be a poet, and he never got two lines to be happy together." That may be the truth. But there will be several other truths. One is, I didn't know it. I thought I was OK, and maybe better. Another truth is that maybe one of these students of mine will be a giant, and I'll have helped him or her. Maybe someone else, a friend or just someone else, will get a whiff of my dedication and because that person has the talent I don't have he or she will make important poems. I don't live in a test tube. To use Williams's figure, I live in a contagious hospital.

*Can I get back to the woman's thing?*

I'd guess nothing could stop you.

*Do you think women should or need to write different poetry from men?*

If they lead very different lives I think they will. I don't know a hell of a lot about women that distinguishes them from men, except for the obvious. I have no sisters. I'm not close to my mother. My grandmother was a small, petty woman, very conservative. I don't see much of my aunts. I have a lot of very close friends who are women, but I don't think those friendships are very different from the ones I have with men. Jean Valentine is a close friend of mine. I sometimes think of her as my sister. She has an astonishing face. When she's happy she can light up a room, and in that way she reminds me of Galway Kinnell. I love both of them. If I were to lose either one I'd feel diminished, smaller, poorer. I've made a lot of close friendships with the women who were my students, and maybe I'm stupid but those friendships don't seem any different than those I made with my male students.

*But the things women live with are different. They're in the kitchen, they're having and raising children, they're cleaning the house, gardening, doing the laundry.*

Men are oiling their rifles, changing flat tires, beating each other with bicycle chains, fixing the sinks of the world, watching the NFL. I don't want to read about all that shit. Do you? Do you want poems about doing the ironing or mowing the lawn? I suppose a good poet can make poetry about the dullest things we do. I believe that underneath these common, ordinary moments the great movements of our lives go on—we grow, we love, we believe, we open our hearts, we close our doors, we give birth, we kill others, we kill ourselves, we embrace each other. I don't know if there, where our great poems will come from, men and women are very different. I'm not saying they're not. I just don't know. It does seem to me that when a poet insists on being intensely masculine or feminine in a poem, as Edna Millay often did or Bukowski does now, the poems seem easy. Elizabeth Bishop is a woman, obviously, but how seldom she insists on it. Even in that incredible poem in the waiting room where reading the *National Geographic* she discovers she's a girl, an

Elizabeth, and she will grow into a woman, it seems she's writing a universal poem, and that a boy could have had exactly that experience and discovered that somehow he was a Robert and would grow into a man. What a poet she is! She's enormous.

*Would you mind being a women? If you were how would you want to write?*

I'd feel odd in skirts. I don't think most people my age want to change sex or gender, whatever they've got. They've grown used to being what they are. But if I were a woman I'd want to write like Whitman, Williams, Bishop, Blake, Chaucer.

*It wouldn't change anything?*

It would probably change everything, but I have no idea what the changes would be. Ask my wife. But don't tell me the answer. I'd be proud to be a woman of independence and courage, to be one of the many women I know. But the actual job that faces me is to become a decent man.

*Do you think you'll make it?*

I'll do my best and hope it's good enough. To mention my beloved Williams again; do you remember the end of his sparrow poem? The male sparrow is hurled aside by the female, falls into the street below and gets run over by a car. The flattened remains seem to say, "I was here. I was a sparrow. I did my best." You can put that on my gravestone.

## UNDER DISCUSSION
### Donald Hall, General Editor

Volumes in the Under Discussion series collect reviews and essays about individual poets. The series is concerned with contemporary American and English poets about whom the consensus has not yet been formed and the final vote has not been taken. Titles in the series include:

**Elizabeth Bishop and Her Art**
*edited by Lloyd Schwartz and Sybil P. Estess*
**Richard Wilbur's Creation** *edited and with an*
*Introduction by Wendy Salinger*
**Reading Adrienne Rich**
*edited by Jane Roberta Cooper*
**On the Poetry of Allen Ginsberg**
*edited by Lewis Hyde*
**Robert Bly: When Sleepers Awake**
*edited by Joyce Peseroff*

Forthcoming volumes will examine the work of Robert Creeley, H.D., Galway Kinnell, and Louis Simpson, among others.

*Please write for further information on available editions and current prices.*

*Ann Arbor*  **The University of Michigan Press**